Sigrun Rittrich-Dorenkamp

Canaries

How to Keep Them
Feeding Them Correctly
Understanding Their Behavior

Photographs: Uwe Anders
Illustrations: Renate Holzner

BARRON'S

CONTENTS

1. What You Should Know Before You Buy

The History of Canaries 8
Natural Environment 8
Getting Ready to Mate 10
The Development of the Young 13
The History of the Harz Roller 17

Considerations 18
Questions to Help You Decide 18
Canaries and Other Pets 22
When You Are Away from Home 23

Legal Questions Related to Keeping Canaries 24
Laws Affecting Tenants 24
Lost-and-Found Birds 25

What to Look for When Buying Canaries 26
Where You Can Get Canaries 26
When to Buy 28
Is the Bird Healthy? 30
The Trip Home 31

Canary Varieties and Colors 32
Responsible Breeding 32
Song Canaries 34
Color Canaries 37
Hybrids 39
Type Canaries 39

2. Proper Conditions and Care

Things Canaries Need 44
Cage Accessories 46
The Aviary 49

Living with Canaries 50
Flying Free 52
The Bird Tree 54
Night Rest 57

A Varied Diet 58
The Basic Food 58
Treats and Extras 62
Drinking Water 65

Conscientious Care 66
Keeping the Cage Clean 67
The Molt 70

Diseases and Preventive Measures 72
Recognizing Illnesses 72
First Aid 77
How to Give Medication 80

Canary Breeding 82
Courtship and Mating 85
Incubation 87
Development of the Chicks 87

3 Understanding Canaries

What Canaries Can Do 92
- The Senses 92
- How Canaries Fly 93
- How Canaries Sing 96
- Body Language 97

Building Trust 100
- Transition to the New Home 100
- Hand-taming Canaries 101
- Getting Canaries Used to Each Other 104
- Canaries and Children 105

Fun and Games with Canaries 106
- Keeping Your Canaries Occupied 106
- Building a Swing 109
- Watching the Birds 110

Solving Problems 112
- Fighting Cocks 112
- Adding a New Bird 113
- Feather Plucking 114
- Abandoning the Nest 115
- If a Song Canary Stops Singing 116
- Escaping 116
- Faded Plumage 117

General Information

My Canary 118

Index 120

Useful Addresses and Literature 125

Information 126

Important Note 127

Children's Corner

Singing 15

The Canary Cage 52

Tasting Your Food 65

Washing 89

Falling Off the Perch 95

Petting 102

A Bird Ladder 111

Naming Canaries 114

What You Should Know Before You Buy

In 1478 the Spanish conquered the Canary Islands. The wild canary was brought back to Spain in large numbers and became the most popular caged bird.

WHAT YOU SHOULD KNOW BEFORE YOU BUY

The History of Canaries

If you have ever visited the Canary Islands, you will have looked in vain for the little, brightly colored yellow or red birds we all think of when we hear the word canary. Flocks of canaries still roam over the islands today, but these wild birds are much more drab than our selectively bred cage birds.

Natural Environment

The Canary Islands, a group of Spanish islands in the Atlantic Ocean about 62 miles (100 km) off the coast of northwestern Africa, are the homeland of canaries. The climate here is even and mild because the Gulf Stream keeps the air from getting too hot or too cold. Daytime temperatures range from 69 to 84°F (21 to 29°C) during the year, and drop an average of only about 5 degrees at night.

The volcanic islands jut out of the deep sea to a height of over 10,000 feet (3,000 m). Mountains,

Is every feather in its proper place? Canaries preen, or groom, themselves with great care.

THE WILD RELATIVES

forests, deep ravines, hidden valleys, hills covered with dense shrubs and bushy succulents, laurel and pine woods, vineyards, meadows, gardens, and parks offer the small songbirds on Grand Canary, Tenerife, Gomera, La Palma, and Hierro an ideal habitat. There are good reasons why ever since antiquity this archipelago has been described as the "islands of the happy ones" or the "happy isles." Canaries are also found on the nearby Madeira Islands and in the Azores, as well as on Cape Verde. On the semiarid eastern Canary Islands of Fuerteventura and Lanzarote, however, the vegetation is not lush enough to support canaries.

The Wild Relatives

From summer until winter, wild canaries range over open landscapes dotted with bushes and trees, gathering in flocks of 50 or more birds and moving in swift, undulating flight. Their olive green plumage streaked with grayish brown provides excellent camouflage and makes them hard to spot among the leaves, branches, and flowers of the vegetation. The wild canary measures slightly over 4.7 inches (12 cm) and is thus a bit smaller than most of our canary breeds, but all the different kinds of canaries in our cages are descended from this wild bird.

This feels wonderful! A refreshing bath is an essential part of the daily grooming.

WHAT YOU SHOULD KNOW BEFORE YOU BUY

The habitat of the wild canary extends from the seacoast to altitudes of almost 6,600 feet (2,000 m). The birds travel over great distances in search of special treats. At harvesttime they like to descend on orchards and gardens to feast on berries and fruit, and especially on figs.

The basic diet of wild canaries throughout the year consists of all kinds of seeds containing oils and starches. These are eaten at various stages of ripeness. But the birds' favorite food is canary seed. They also eat the seeds of other grasses and of plants belonging to the daisy and mustard families (Compositae and Cruciferae), as well as of plantain, knotweed, poppy, chickweed, and some millet varieties. In addition, they like to pick out the seeds of sugarcane, and in the spring they nibble on young leaf and flower buds.

At the end of the mild winters, the flocks disband. Canaries do not breed in colonies. Older pairs that have raised young in a past season sometimes return to their old nests. By this time, the previous year's offspring already have their adult plumage and start looking for mates of their own.

Getting Ready to Mate

Finding a good place to raise

Fresh dandelion leaves are irresistible. Canaries consider them a great delicacy, and they are high in vitamins.

GETTING READY TO MATE

a family is not at all easy. The preferred location for a nest is in an isolated tree or rather large bush, which, ideally, has a branch protruding about 7 to 10 feet (2 to 3 m) from the ground to serve as a singing perch. From here, the male will sing his song, thus vocally declaring his territory. When the breeding season starts in February or early March, the song becomes

WHAT YOU SHOULD KNOW BEFORE YOU BUY

The Wild Ancestor of the Canary

Scientific Name	Canaries belong to the family of finches (Fringillidae, subfamily Carduelinae) and to the genus *Serinus*. The scientific name of the canary is *Serinus canaria*.
Size	With an overall length of about 4.9 inches (12.5 cm), the wild canary is smaller than many selectively bred strains. Color canaries are slightly longer, and type canaries range from 4.3 to 9 inches (11 to 23 cm).
Plumage	Olive green with dark, brownish gray streaking above, and dark tail and wing feathers. Males are more brightly colored on throat, breast, and abdomen than the grayish green females.
Behavior	Wild canaries live in social groups during the second half of the year, gathering in flocks of up to 50 birds. From January to March they form pair bonds, and males become intolerant of each other. Canaries breed in individual pairs. They travel across great distances on the islands.
Related Birds	The closest relative of our canary is the wild canary, or serin (*Serinus serinus*). Other relatives are various siskins and green finches.

louder and more persistent. The cocks now sing from dawn to dusk, each seeking to attract a female and drive away other males. If song fails to deter a rival, the matter escalates into pecking fights and sorties in pursuit of the intruder.

Courtship display flights are also accompanied by song. The song stimulates the nest-building instinct in the female. The more melodious the male's song, the more diligently the female works at weaving the cup-shaped nest out of grasses, thin stems and twigs, dry leaves, and moss. The best spot for a nest is a forked branch about 10 feet (3 m) off the ground or in a thick bush. When the basic structure is completed, the inside is lined with feathers and soft fibers. Soon after the nest is finished, the female lays three to five pale blue eggs, but she does not start

A red canary cock is feeding his mate as a sign of affection.

THE DEVELOPMENT OF THE YOUNG

TIP

In nature it is not uncommon for a pair of canaries to produce three clutches and raise as many as 15 young in one breeding season. Caged canaries will also breed up to three times in succession, but you should not allow this to happen because it puts too much strain on the female.

sitting on them until the clutch is complete. From this point on, the male feeds his mate so that she will not have to get off the nest too often. The pair do not take turns brooding the eggs.

After 13 to 14 days all the chicks hatch at the same time. They crack the shell from the inside with the *egg tooth*, a small protrusion at the tip of the upper mandible. The baby birds start breathing even before they emerge from the shell.

Newly hatched they are almost completely naked and keep their eyes closed. Because there is a

little yolk left in the yolk sack within the abdominal cavity, the chicks need no food on the day they hatch.

The Development of the Young

Once the chicks have hatched, it is the male adult's job to provide sufficient food. He continues to feed the female and also brings food for the babies.

During the rearing phase canaries require extra protein, which they get in the form of small insects, beetles, caterpillars, and aphids. This menu is supplemented with plenty of greens and with figs. For the first few days the female usually feeds the young by herself with a mush of twice predigested food. Soon the male, too, starts stuffing the ever demanding little beaks with predigested food from his crop.

The young grow very fast. After a mere 15 days the plumage is essentially complete, and the stubby tail and the downy feathers on the head remain the only signs of the birds' tender age. They will leave the nest soon now, but the parents will go on feeding them for about another ten days. The father often takes complete charge of providing for them at this stage, and he

1
WHAT YOU SHOULD KNOW BEFORE YOU BUY

also teaches them to forage and eat on their own.

The canary mother starts getting ready for the next brood. If the weather cooperates, being neither too hot nor too dry nor too cold, a third clutch is often produced. Under favorable conditions a pair of canaries can raise as many as 12 or even 15 young in one year.

After the breeding season the parent birds together with their offspring gather once again in flocks and travel back and forth across the islands.

How the "Golden Birds" Came to Us

The Spanish who conquered and occupied the Canary Islands over 500 years ago, from 1478 to 1496, were taken with these pretty yellowish green birds who sang so sweetly. Soldiers and sailors brought the little songsters home as pre-

The head is not easy to get at. In order to scratch, a canary raises its leg between the body and the wing.

HOW THE "GOLDEN BIRDS" CAME TO US

Do All Canaries Sing Well?

All male canaries can sing, but not all of them sing equally well. Song canaries undergo special training. They attend "singing school" in the fall, when they are about six months old. At that point the breeder places them singly in small cages, the so-called song cages, for a few weeks so that they will not be distracted from learning. The young cocks see no other birds but only hear them. A good singing tutor is provided; in Belgium this model singer is even called "Teacher." The young cocks try to imitate his song as best they can. Practicing diligently, they learn several phrases by heart, and anything they have once learned they will never forget.

cious, rare gifts. Canaries, also called "sugar birds" because of their liking for sweet things, quickly became fashionable. They became a symbol of luxury and cosmopolitanism, and their price skyrocketed to the point where only the wealthy could afford to buy them. It did not take the sailors long to realize that good money could be made selling canaries, and they kept bringing back more and more of them. But sea travel, which was slow and dangerous in those days, took a heavy toll on the little birds.

Spanish monks, meanwhile, tried to breed canaries in their monasteries. Their efforts soon met with success, and the monks were able to develop a flourishing trade in birds they bred.

Before long, canaries were sold not only in Spain but also in Italy, France, and England. Being shrewd business men, the Spanish monks sold only male birds and in this way established a monopoly, which they were able to maintain for almost 100 years, but toward the end of the sixteenth century, canary breeding was taken up in Italy, and not much later, in England and France as well.

It is still a mystery how the Spanish monks' monopoly was broken. Perhaps some female canaries were exported by mistake since the sexes are not easy to tell apart in the fall and winter. Or perhaps someone, in exchange for a sufficiently large bribe, smuggled some canary hens out of the country.

WHAT YOU SHOULD KNOW BEFORE YOU BUY

In Italy canary breeding spread slowly from the south northward. This happened gradually enough so that the warmth-loving birds were able to adjust to the colder weather and greater temperature fluctuations of central and northern Europe.

Tyrol, the western region of Austria in the Alps, now became the primary center of canary breeding. The miners of that area realized that the birds could provide them with a reliable second income. Their breeding goal was to produce birds that combined beautiful song with bright colors. They developed yellow and pied strains, and there were some white canaries even at that early stage. The Tyroleans also hit on the idea of keeping nightingales as tutors for the young canary cocks. This is how canaries learned to imitate the song of nightingales. The more melodious, the higher the price.

Demand for canaries kept growing throughout Europe, including countries as far away as Russia and Turkey.

Tyrolean canary breeding reached its peak in the eighteenth century. A German operetta, *The Bird Peddler* (*Der Vogelhändler*), is set in this period.

TIP

When buying a canary, check the cage where the canary you have chosen is kept. Is the cage clean, and do all the other birds in it look well taken care of and alert? If the answer is no, you should find another pet shop or breeder. Buy your birds before noon so that they will have enough time to adjust to their new home while there is daylight.

Almost 100 years ago, breeders succeeded in crossbreeding canaries with a hooded siskin from Venezuela. Before that there were no red canaries.

THE HISTORY OF THE HARZ ROLLER

One baby bird has hatched and is being fed by the mother with predigested food from her crop.

The History of the Harz Roller

In the nineteenth century the Harz Mountains in central Germany developed into a mining center, and many miners from the Tyrol moved there, attracted by the new job opportunities. They naturally brought along their canaries.

In the Harz region, especially in a town called Sankt Andreasberg, the Tyrolean miners started breeding canaries.

The Harz Roller acquired world fame. It was in great demand all over Europe, and starting in 1842 these canaries were also shipped to America. By 1860 over 15,000 Rollers were sold in North America annually, and in 1882 over 120,000 were sent to New York. In the years around the turn of the century over a million Harz Rollers were exported, and even today the word canary still conjures up for many people the picture of a yellow, honey-voiced Harz Roller.

WHAT YOU SHOULD KNOW BEFORE YOU BUY

Considerations

Anyone wishing to have canaries should first consider carefully whether he or she will be able to provide the kind of conditions and care these sociable songbirds need to be happy.

Questions to Help You Decide

1 A male canary will sing whenever the mood strikes and for as long as he feels like it. Having to listen to the song can become tiresome. On the other hand, canaries often don't sing at all during the molt, a physiological process that takes a lot out of the birds. Then again, your canary might stop singing for good. Will you still love it if that should happen?

2 If kept properly, canaries can live as long as 10 to 15 years. Are you prepared to assume such a long-term responsibility?

3 Do you have enough time to devote to canaries? The birds have to be fed and cared for every day. They will remain healthy and cheerful only if they get a varied diet, are kept clean, and are watched closely for any sign of trouble.

4 Who will look after the birds when you want to go away or if you get sick and have to go to the hospital (see page 23)?

5 Canaries are sociable creatures. Are you able to keep several birds or at least a pair? It is true, of course, that a single bird becomes more attached to its keeper, but would you be able to keep it company whenever it yearns for a partner? If not, the bird would languish and possibly die of loneliness.

6 Do you have enough space for a large cage or, better yet, an indoor aviary (see page 49)?

7 If you are thinking of getting canaries for your child, keep in mind that a child's interest can wane quickly. Then it would be up to you to see to it that the canaries get the care they need (see page 105).

8 Canaries that don't live in an aviary should have a chance at least once a day to fly free in the room. When they do, they may leave a few droppings

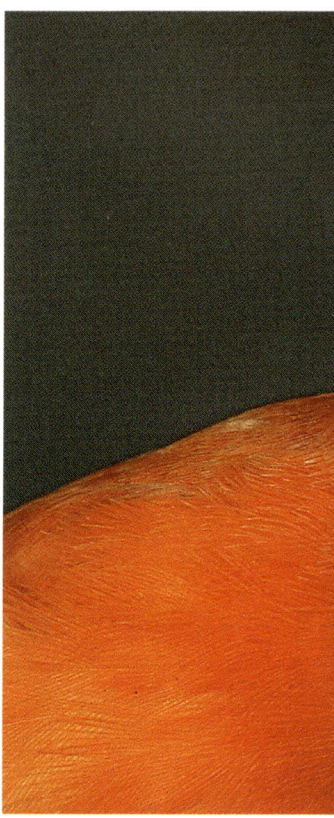

Rubbing bills is a sign of mutual sympathy—for the birds, the color is irrelevant.

MALE OR FEMALE?

behind. Can you put up with this?

9 Seeds may land on the floor around the cage or aviary. Will the mess upset you?

10 Have you made sure that no one in your family is allergic to feathers or feather dust (see Important Note, page 127)?

Male or Female?
Ideally you should keep both male and female birds. If your main interest is to have a bird that sings well, you should definitely choose a male song canary. Only they produce proper songs consisting of several phrases. Hens (the technical term for female birds) are very

1 WHAT YOU SHOULD KNOW BEFORE YOU BUY

Great job! Before the female starts brooding the eggs, they are duly admired.

quiet. Generally, they only chirp softly now and then. That doesn't mean that they are incapable of song; they simply have no reason to sing. After all, the cock sings to establish his territory, attract a mate, and do his part during the brooding period.

If, on the other hand, song doesn't matter to you very much and you are more intrigued with the colors and shapes of canaries, you will derive just as much pleasure from a hen.

Determining the sex of canaries is not easy outside of the breeding season. There is hardly any exterior difference between males and females. In wild canaries, the female is more drab than the male, but in our selectively bred birds the hen is often just as brightly colored as the cock. Song is the best indicator of gender. But young cocks

PLEASE, NO SOLITARY CONFINEMENT!

> **TIP** ▼
>
> Breeders can reliably tell the sex of a canary during the courtship period. They pick the bird up carefully, turn it upside down, and gently blow the feathers around the vent to one side. In a cock the vent is swollen and sticks up; in females, the vent is flat.

don't start singing until late summer or fall, and older ones take a rest from singing while they molt.

What Variety of Canary?

Contrary to popular conception, not all canaries are yellow and gifted singers.

Only the so-called song canaries (see page 34) conform to this picture. In addition to song canaries there are color canaries, which are constantly gaining in popularity (see page 37), and type canaries (see page 39).

All varieties of canaries can sing, but the voice of color and type canaries is usually louder and shriller. The song of Harz Rollers and other specialized singers is much softer and more melodious.

What variety you choose is entirely a matter of personal taste. Color canaries, song canaries, and type canaries that are small and sleek are suitable for beginners. Large varieties and frilled birds, or ones with a bent posture, are not suitable for a cage in the living room and should be kept only by expert fanciers.

Please, No Solitary Confinement!

Birds are social animals and should never be kept singly.

■ No matter how hard you try, you can't make up for the lack of a proper partner for your canary. You can't be there for your bird all the time, and, left alone, it will feel lonely and frustrated. This can give rise to a variety of psychological problems as well as physical sickness. It is possible for birds to die from melancholy and loneliness.

■ Unfortunately, many people, hoping to prevent their birds from being distracted from singing, still keep canary cocks singly in cages that are much too small. The fact is that cocks sing even if they live in large cages together with other canaries; they just don't sing quite as much. Keeping birds singly violates their natural needs.

■ Canaries can engage in their natural social behavior only if at least two birds live together. A pair is also much more interesting and fun to observe than a single bird. If you are worried about unwanted offspring, this can

WHAT YOU SHOULD KNOW BEFORE YOU BUY

be prevented by removing all nesting materials from the cage.

■ Two or more females can be kept together without problems. However, several males should be combined only if your aviary is big enough so that each of them can establish a territory. Otherwise, they will compete with each other and fight constantly, at least during the first half of the year, and the subordinate birds will eventually succumb.

■ In a large aviary you can keep a number of canaries, but the birds will not become as friendly and tame as canaries kept singly or in pairs.

Canaries and Other Pets

A *dog* can usually be taught not to bother birds and will learn to accept them as members of the family. But don't leave your dog alone with them at the beginning.

A *cat* can only rarely be trained to overcome its instinct to try to catch birds.

Rodents like hamsters, guinea pigs, chinchillas, and rabbits can coexist in the same household without problems. But caution is in order with rats; they can harm canaries.

An *aquarium* is not dangerous as long as it is completely covered. If there is any uncovered area, a canary can fall in the tank and drown.

Other small birds can usually be combined with canaries without causing any difficulties because canaries are not aggressive by nature. But you do have to have a very large cage or a sizable aviary. Closely related birds, such as the serin (*Serinus serinus*) and the European

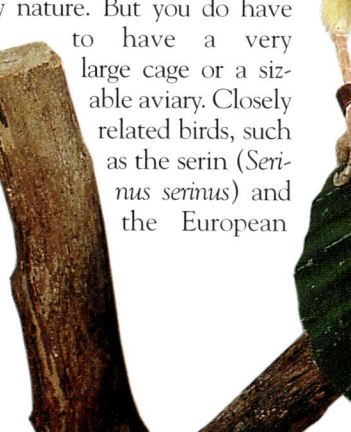

Fresh, juicy food—in this case a slice of cucumber—is appreciated by all canaries.

WHEN YOU ARE AWAY FROM HOME

What the Bird-sitter Has to Know

Food	What kind of food and how much the birds get. Where the food is kept and how it is prepared. What kind of greens and fruit the birds like. Feeding times.
Chores	What chores have to be done daily—for example: giving fresh water, cleaning the bird bath. What has to be done weekly—for example: replacing the sand, scrubbing the perches.
Behavior	How should the caretaker interact with the canaries? What should he or she watch out for when the birds fly free (e.g., possible dangers)?
Addresses	Telephone number and address of the avian veterinarian. The address and telephone number where you can be reached.

goldfinch (*Carduelis carduelis*), get along well with canaries, as do some more distantly related finches. It is not a good idea to keep canaries with parakeets or cockatiels. These larger birds of the parrot family tend to attack with beak and claws, against which the small songsters are defenseless.

When You Are Away from Home

Your canaries are happiest at home, in their accustomed surroundings. That is why you should look for a reliable bird-sitter in good time in case you want to go away or will not be able to get home for more than two days. If you can't find a reliable person to come to your home during your absence, ask around if there is someone who could keep your birds. Sometimes pet stores or veterinary offices are willing to take in birds for short periods, or a breeder may agree to house your canaries temporarily. Or you might find a boarding place for pets where the personnel is knowledgeable about birds.

WHAT YOU SHOULD KNOW BEFORE YOU BUY

Legal Questions Related to Keeping Canaries

Laws Affecting Tenants

If your lease says nothing about keeping pets you may go on the assumption that ordinary pets are permitted. Pets have become a normal part of modern life and keeping them is included in the use of an apartment as long as they cause no problems. This is particularly true for small cage birds, which by their nature are unlikely to cause problems. Keeping them is not associated with significant smell, nor are they noisy enough to disturb neighbors, and they are too small to do much damage in an apartment. Thus, no explicit permission from the landlord is needed to keep canaries. *Things become problematical*, however, when one or two canaries evolve into a breeding flock consisting of a large number of birds. Here, the specific situation has to be evaluated to determine if there is reason for legal complaint. According to some legal experts, the keeping of "an excessive number" of pets constitutes such reason, as does the plugging up of pipes because bird sand or litter was flushed down the toilet.

Condominiums

A blanket ban on the keeping of canaries has legal force only if all the members of the condominium community decide on it by unanimous consent. A mere majority is often not sufficient to forbid the keeping of pets. However, a majority vote can limit to "a reasonable number" the pets kept in a condominium.

Breeding

No permit is needed to breed canaries.

Protection of Species

Canaries, which are a domesticated form of their wild ancestor, are not subject to any regulations enacted to protect endangered species.

Purchase Contracts

It is customary these days that any reputable dealer will supply the buyer with a detailed purchase agreement that should include the date of purchase, the price paid, and the addresses of both seller and buyer. The sex of the bird should also be mentioned if this is important to the buyer. Anyone buying a canary is entering into a purchase contract with the seller.

If it turns out after the canary is handed over that there is something wrong with it (for instance, the bird is sick), the buyer can assert the right of warranty and either cancel the purchase or get a full refund. The condition for such a step is, of course, that the bird was already sick at the time it was sold. Especially in the case of infectious diseases, it is difficult to determine the onset of illness, and the question can generally be settled only by a competent veterinarian. If a buyer wants to make use of the warranty provision, he or she has to do so within a

LEGAL QUESTIONS

certain time, as indicated on the warranty paper(s) or contract.

Parents should think twice before buying a canary. Children who are less than eight years old usually want an animal primarily to hug and pet, and perhaps are pleading for a dog. You should not buy a canary as a gesture of compromise in this situation. Even the tamest canary cannot possibly satisfy a child's need for physical contact with an animal. A young child might squeeze the bird affectionately and unintentionally cause its death. No warranty papers or contracts can help you if this happens.

Lost-and-Found Birds

If you come across a canary that has escaped, the proper action is to treat it as a lost-and-found object. Contact your local police, animal shelter, bird club, and/or place a lost-and-found ad in the local paper.

If your bird manages to fly out of your home and escapes, place an ad in the local paper (don't forget to include your phone number, and you might consider offering a small reward to anyone finding the bird).

The drinking water has to be fresh at all times. Water contaminated with droppings can give rise to serious diseases.

25

1 WHAT YOU SHOULD KNOW BEFORE YOU BUY

What to Look for When Buying Canaries

You should take plenty of time when you buy birds that will share your home with you. Canaries are available in great numbers and in many varieties. Making a careful choice will save you disappointment later on.

Where You Can Get Canaries

There are several different ways of acquiring canaries.

■ Good pet stores sell canaries of many different kinds. The male birds are often kept in separate cages and try to outdo each other singing, so you will have a chance to compare their musical abilities on the spot.

In a pet store you can also get a cage and accessories, along with the right kind of food, when you purchase your birds.

■ You can also buy directly from a breeder. However, most breeders specialize in one particular variety of

Canaries spend several hours a day thoroughly grooming their plumage.

WHERE YOU CAN GET CANARIES

Fighting over the best spot at the melon. He who screams the loudest may end up the winner.

canary and, within that variety, in a few colors or shapes. Consequently, you rarely get an overview of the many different varieties of canaries there are.

On the other hand, there are many special varieties that are never sold by dealers and that you can obtain only from a breeder. Canary breeders are found almost everywhere, and probably there are some near where you live.

You can get addresses of breeders from local bird clubs or from national bird societies (see Addresses, page 125). Breeders as well as ordinary people also often advertise the offspring of their birds in bird magazines and local papers.

■ Breeders exhibit their birds at bird shows. At these shows you can get an overview of the different kinds of canaries as well as get addresses of breeders. You may even be able to set up an appointment with a breeder then and there.

■ In many areas there are monthly animal auctions. Sometimes breeders sell their birds there.

■ If you have friends or relatives that keep canaries and if the birds breed, you will probably be welcome to take some of the offspring.

Note: I strongly advise against purchasing canaries by mail. The frightened birds are under great stress while being shipped, and if you are unlucky, the delivery man may hand you a sick bird or one that has expired.

1 WHAT YOU SHOULD KNOW BEFORE YOU BUY

When to Buy

Canaries are, of course, available throughout the year, but *the best time to buy one is the fall, from September to November or early December.* This is when breeders dispose of their birds' offspring, and you will be able to choose from among a great many young canaries.

At this point the birds are five to seven months old and have completed their juvenile molt (see page 70).

Anyone looking for a young songster should, however, wait until November or December. It takes that long for the young cocks to complete their musical training (see page 15).

How Old Should the Bird Be?

Reputable breeders and dealers will not sell canaries before the birds have completed their juvenile molt.

At this point the young canaries are practically

Once all dust has been removed and the feathers are put in order, the plumage is oiled with a secretion from the preen gland.

HOW OLD SHOULD THE BIRD BE?

indistinguishable from their elders and eat without help from their parents.

This is usually the case by September. Depending on the hatching date, the young birds are anywhere from four to six months old then. If they are transferred to a new home any earlier, the adjustment may lead to complications.

Song canaries are still practicing their singing skills at that age. Their "education" is not completed until November or December, when they are about six to eight months old. Older birds generally adjust to a new home without problem.

The age of a canary is easy to tell if the bird has a leg band. The hatching date along with numbers identifying the breeder and the bird club are printed on the band. This closed band or ring can be slipped on a bird's foot only during the first week. Because it cannot be removed later on, the information on it is considered reliable; however, not all canaries wear bands.

Unlike birds of the parrot family, canaries are not required to wear bands, but all registered canary breeders band their young birds.

If a canary has no band, it is very hard to tell whether you are looking at a young or an old bird. Only the feet give some clue. In the first year the skin is smooth and soft;

A canary about to take off. From this kind of perch it can leap into the air with ease.

WHAT YOU SHOULD KNOW BEFORE YOU BUY

later it turns somewhat rough and scaly.

Is the Bird Healthy?

You can usually tell at a glance if a bird is not feeling well. A sick bird will sit on a perch or even squat on the cage bottom by itself, apathetic and with raised plumage. The head is often tucked under the wing or the eyes are half closed. The feathers around the vent may be soiled with feces, a sign of diarrhea. Or there may be a sticky discharge from the eyes. Step back a little from the cage and watch the canaries quietly for some time. If they sense danger, birds often make an effort to look normal and flatten their plumage even if they are sick, so you might easily be deceived about a bird's state of health.

It is true, of course, that birds also puff up their feathers and hide their heads when they sleep, but healthy canaries sleep at night and only rarely take brief naps in the middle of the day.

If you see a canary that looks like a fluffy ball of feathers in daytime, stay away from it to be on the safe side. However, canaries are generally robust and rarely get sick. An alert and lively bird is probably healthy.

Always wash lettuce leaves well and dry them before giving them to your canaries.

THE TRIP HOME

Health Check at a Glance

	A Healthy Canary	**A Sick Canary**
Plumage	Smooth, shiny, clean, unbroken	Shaggy, puffed up, bare spots
Behavior	Lively, alert; bird interacts with other birds, preens, and picks at the food often	Apathetic, isolated, eyes half closed, head hidden
Eyes/Nostrils	Eyes clear and shiny	Sticky, caked with discharge
Cloaca	Clean, smooth	Red, feathers around it soiled with feces
Breast	Breastbone rounded	Breast sunken, breastbone sticks out sharply
Legs	Horny scales form smooth surface, feet and toes clean and straight, three toes point forward, one back	Thickened skin, scabs, cracks, very scaly, toes deformed or partially missing
Droppings	Mushy to solid and dark; uric acid clearly separate, white, and semisolid	Runny, greenish

The Trip Home

If the trip from the breeder or the pet shop to your home is a short one you can safely take the bird along in a small cardboard box with some air holes. Dealers generally supply such boxes of folded cardboard (see photo, page 46).

If you carry your box carefully and make sure it won't go flying through the car if you should have to slam on the brakes, your newly acquired canary will arrive in its new home safe and sound. For a longer journey, use wooden shipping boxes with a small window grate.

It is important to make your canaries' adjustment to their new home as easy as possible so that they will learn to trust you.

WHAT YOU SHOULD KNOW BEFORE YOU BUY

Canary Varieties and Colors

Of the approximately 500 different color variations, five are represented on this perch.

Most people still think of the canary as a small yellow bird that can sing well. Yet today there are about 130 different canary breeds and over 500 different color variations. All of them are descended from the quite inconspicuous wild canary.

Responsible Breeding

In the course of over 500 years breeders have turned the small wild birds into creatures of civilization, into domestic animals that have little in common with their wild ancestor. What they have created does not always meet with the approval of animal lovers, but their labors are appreciated by a large circle of enthusiastic fanciers. As long as selective breeding causes no impairment of life functions and the birds are healthy and lively and do not suffer, nonexperts should refrain from criticism. To argue that these birds could not survive in nature is beside the point. They were, after all, created to live under human care. In their guidelines for breeding, canary breeders' organizations specifically state their opposition to traits that "affect biological functions negatively." Where the birds' viability is threatened, as when the birds' resistance is lowered, when feathers that are too soft form cysts, or when legs that are too straight give rise to joint problems, further intensive breeding of the strains in question should be rejected. The School of Veterinary Medicine at the University of Hannover, Germany, is currently conducting studies to determine whether the skeletons of exaggerated types, such as the Gibber Italicus (see photo, page 40), exhibit detrimental anatomical changes.

Canary lovers play an important role in shaping the demand for birds and thus affect whether breeders concentrate on creating more and more outlandish variations or on producing healthy and lively canaries.

The several hundred strains of canaries are generally classified into three large groups: birds bred for their voice, their color, or their shape. There are also innumerable crossbreedings of different strains.

RESPONSIBLE BREEDING

WHAT YOU SHOULD KNOW BEFORE YOU BUY

Above, left: The Harz or Roller Canary is the best known of the song canaries.

Above, right: A bird of the color variety orange-red-agate.

Photo on page 35, below: The bird on the right is a capped or cap-marked canary, which also shows some variegation on other parts of its body; the bird on the left is a pastel-orange-red mutation.

Song Canaries

All canaries can sing, but not all of them have beautiful voices. Canary cocks use their song to discourage rivals acoustically from infringing on their territory. But canaries are also capable of imitating the voices of other birds.

The Harz Roller is the most famous "feathered chamber singer." It originated in the last century in Germany's Harz Mountains (see page 17), but today it is bred all over the world.

The Harz Roller is yellow. Centuries of selective breeding have refined its song so that it is pleasant to listen to, melodious, varied, and sung through an apparently closed beak. This breed's song is made up primarily of four types of phrases or "tours," as the experts call them. They are the hollow roll, the base roll, the flute, and the hollow bell. The hollow roll is the most important element of the song. The bird sings a rolled "r" in combination with the vowels "o" (as in gold) or "u" (as in Lulu). The hollow roll sounds something like "rururu." For the base roll

SONG CANARIES

A hybrid (mule) involving a canary and another species (in this case a hooded siskin).

Above right: A pastel-orange-red-agate-pastel mutation.

the bird lowers its voice, and the resulting low-pitched "rourourou" is particularly prized. The hollow bell is produced through the combination of the consonant "l" with the vowels. The bird sings "lülülü" or "lololo," down to a low-pitched "lululu." In the flute there are separate soft but clear notes that start with a "d" and sound like "du" or "dou." They often occur at the conclusion of a concert. If the singer incorporates the vowel "e" (as in beet), experts call this a bell tour.

The Waterslager, also called Belgian Waterslager, is somewhat larger than the Harz Roller and light yellow in color. This breed's song has a beating sound unlike the soft, rolling song of the Harz Roller.

35

WHAT YOU SHOULD KNOW BEFORE YOU BUY

The *Spanish Timbrado* is still quite unknown here. It resembles the wild canary in appearance, and its song is reminiscent of small bells ringing.

The *American Singer* was developed in the United States. The breeders were trying to combine the features of all three major classes of canaries. The

Above, left: This pretty variety is called yellow-agate-yellow-ivory.

Above, right: Two slate-colored birds.

COLOR CANARIES

Above, left: Here an Alanio serin and a canary were paired.

Above, right: A pair of canary serins. This is what the wild ancestors of our cage birds look like.

Below, right: The parents of this bird were a red-capped serin and a canary.

Page 36, below: A silver-brown-satinette canary flanked by a red and a yellow canary.

American Singer sings well, in the style of the Harz Roller, is brightly colored like the color canaries, and has soft feathers and a good posture, in this respect resembling many type canaries.

American Singers are still hard to find in other parts of the world.

Color Canaries

Color canaries can, of course, sing just like other canaries, but they were not bred with the aim of refining their voices. The breeders of color canaries concentrated more on producing new shades and achieving uniformity of color. Originally, canaries were a rather drab olive green with grayish brown to brownish black wing and tail feathers and with dark streaking on the upper side. Only the breast and abdomen sported some brighter color. When mutations (sudden genetic changes) caused the loss of some of the dark pigments or melanins,

37

WHAT YOU SHOULD KNOW BEFORE YOU BUY

the first variegated or pied canaries were born. With the loss of all the melanins, the birds became completely yellow. The green color too disappeared. The markings and feathers that had been dark now were white.

"Light" or "lipochrome" is the term experts use to describe these canaries that lack melanins. The most typical example is the yellow canary. This color is "lipochrome," which means fat color. There is also a red fat color. When not only the melanins disappear but the fat colors as well, the birds appear pure white.

Breeders have developed hundreds of different shades by combining lipochrome birds colored yellow, red, or white with canaries retaining the original dark colors or melanins. In some varieties, the markings show up prominently; in others, they are muted, and in still others, only a hint of them remains.

Melanin canaries are now subdivided into black, brown, agate, and isabel birds, and in some other varieties the original streaking remains only as a faint shadow.

Breeders also discovered that some birds had shorter feathers in which the colors appear intensified. Breeders

Above, left: Crossings of canaries with scarlet grosbeaks and bullfinches produce very handsome hybrids.

Above, right: Black siskins and canaries were the parents of these hybrids.

Photo on right: The Border Fancy (on the left) looks like a ball of feathers. The Fife Fancy (on the right) is a small, round, smooth type canary.

TYPE CANARIES

Above, left: This type canary is a German Crest.

Above, right: The Gloster Corona is one of the most popular crested canaries.

called these "intensive" or "A" birds. In other varieties a whitish rim on the feathers tones down the color. These birds are called "non-intensive" or "B" canaries.

Hybrids

Some breeders try to create new colors by crossing canaries with other, closely related species. This often results in very pretty hybrids. The interbreeding of canaries and other serins shows particular promise. European breeders also often mate male *Carduelis carduelis* with female canaries. The offspring are beautifully colored; however, many of them are sterile.

Type Canaries

Breeders of type canaries concentrate on the shape and overall appearance of the birds. Experts distinguish between smooth, bent, and frilled canaries. At this time, there are 26 different kinds of type canaries.

Very arched and frilled breeds are the most arresting

39

WHAT YOU SHOULD KNOW BEFORE YOU BUY

looking of the type canaries. Among these are the Gibber Italicus (see photo, bottom right), the Southern Dutch Frill, the Makige, the Swiss Frill, and the Giboso Español. Some of these extremes of selective breeding are supposed to resemble the number 7 or even the number 1 in their posture and stand on legs stretched straight.

Among the smooth arched breeds is the Belgian Bult, 6.7 inches (17 cm), which is also supposed to look like the number 7 when standing. The small Japanese Hoso, 4.3 to 4.7 inches (11 to 12 cm), the large Scotch Fancy (at least 6.7 inches [17 cm]; photo, above, left), the Rhinelander, and the Münchener also have a more or less rounded, crescent-shaped back.

Straight, frilled canaries stand up erect and include the Parisian, Padovan, Northern Dutch, Fiorino, and Mehringer Frills. Of these the Parisian Frill (see photo, page 41), measuring 7 to 9 inches (18 to 23 cm), is the largest. The long feathers on the back, head, and

Above, left: The Scotch Fancy, which measures about 6.7 inches (17 cm), is one of the largest type canaries.

Above, right: A Gloster Corona (left) and a Gloster Consort (right).

Photo on left: The Gibber Italicus is a frilled type canary with a curved posture.

TYPE CANARIES

Above, left: The Parisian Frill is special because of its size of 7 to 9 inches (18 to 23 cm) and its impressive curls.

Above, right: Yorkshires are a large variety with dense plumage. They are also exceptionally friendly.

legs are supposed to conform exactly to a precisely defined pattern.

Smooth type canaries, both large and small, are very popular. One of these is the Gloster Corona (see photo, page 40) with its crest that makes it look as though it has bangs. But this canary can only be paired with an uncrested bird, such as the Gloster Consort. Other canaries with fringed crests are the massive Crested Canary, 6.7 inches (17 cm), and the outsized Lancashire, 9 inches (23 cm). These birds too have to be mated with their uncrested equivalents, the Crestbred and the Lancashire Plainhead, respectively. The German Crest (see photo, page 39) is a medium-sized canary. Most of the smooth type canaries come from England. Among them is the Yorkshire (see photo, above, right), which is a favorite in the United States, too. It is a large canary that is very friendly, just like the sturdy Norwich canary, whose plumage is dense and silky. Other smooth breeds are the Border canary, Fife, Raza Española, and Bernese.

Proper Conditions and Care

Healthy canaries are always active during the day. They charm us with their song, cheerful temperament, and pretty colors. If you offer them the proper conditions and care, these small songsters will repay you for your troubles for years to come.

2 PROPER CONDITIONS AND CARE

Things Canaries Need

You should have a large cage or an aviary all equipped and set up in the spot where it is going to stay by the time your new birds arrive. If you still have to do anything in the birds' living quarters when the birds are already there, you will needlessly upset them.

A Comfortable Cage

Because of their ability to fly, birds in the wild are used to almost limitless freedom. That is why a cage should be spacious enough to allow for at least a few wing beats to get from perch to perch. The more room the birds have, the healthier they will be.

Cage size: An ideal cage is about 40 × 24 × 32 inches (100 × 60 × 80 cm). Such a cage is big enough for two canaries. Smaller cages, down to a minimum size of about 24 × 12 × 24 inches (60 × 30 × 60 cm) are acceptable only if the door is left open many hours of the day and the birds can choose when to fly free in the room and when to return to the safety of the cage. These small cages should, however, never be used at all for type canaries, most of which are larger than other canary breeds.

Shape of cage: Rectangular cages are best. When looking at manufacturers' specifications, don't let yourself be tempted by fancy curves and bays. These embellishments are of no use to the birds for flying (see TIP, above).

Cage bars: In the case of canaries it does not matter whether the bars run horizontally or vertically. Canaries don't climb up on them the way cockatiels, for example, do. The space

> **TIP**
>
> Round cages are not suitable for canaries because they offer no points of orientation or corners for retreat. Cages made of wood are not ideal either because they are hard to clean and can become breeding grounds for mites and fungal spores.

Canaries love to splash around in fresh water.

A COMFORTABLE CAGE

A swinging basket like this is pretty exciting. Who will be the first one to get in?

between the bars should measure about ½ inch (12 mm), so the birds can't squeeze through or get stuck between the bars. Canaries don't chew on the cage bars, and you can therefore pick a synthetic finish, preferably in a dark color. A brass or chrome-plated cage may match the living room lamp nicely, but it will reflect light, which is unpleasant for both birds and observers.

Note: If enough light enters from the front, box cages with three solid walls may be a good choice. The birds have more peace and quiet in them and feel less exposed. (An additional benefit of having three solid walls is that dirt can fly out in only one direction.) In regular cages a deep-sided bottom section made of plastic is desirable. It will help contain litter, bits of food, and feathers. A sand drawer is also important because it makes changing the litter easier.

2 PROPER CONDITIONS AND CARE

Cage Accessories

Perches: Commercially available cages usually come complete with three or four perches. There is no need for extra perches, but those provided are almost always made of plastic or wooden dowels. Neither material is ideal.

Replace at least some of the perches with natural wood, such as branches of fruit trees, elderberry bushes, willows, oaks, alder, or poplar. Commercial perches made of plastic or dowels can cause sores on the bottom of the birds' feet. By contrast, the irregular and softer surface of natural branches provides healthful foot exercise. The branches should be of varying diameter with some of them thick enough that the birds' toes reach only about two-thirds or three-quarters of the way around them.

Natural branches are not only better for the birds' feet but are also more pleasant to rub the beak against.

You can gather branches from your garden or from the woods, or you can buy them, cut to size, at pet stores. Scrub them with hot water before mounting them in the cage.

It is important that at least some of the perches be attached in such a way that they give or sway a little. Also, not all of them should

Food dispensers are practical, but they can get plugged up.

A cuttlebone supplies canaries with the calcium that is so important for them.

Water dispensers keep the water from becoming dirty.

CAGE ACCESSORIES

This is what a well-arranged cage looks like. All the food dishes are accessible from the outside.

Photo on page 46, left: A cardboard box like this one lets you transport a canary safely.

be in an horizontal position. After all, very few branches stick out horizontally from trees. To attach them to the cage you can notch the branches with a sharp knife. Often, they can simply be squeezed between two bars. Place the perches in such a way that they don't interfere with the birds' flying. Also make sure that enough space is left between them and the sides of the cage so that the birds' tail feathers will not rub against the bars.

Note: Never use branches from trees that have been sprayed or are next to heavily traveled roads. The traces of pesticides and exhaust fumes are poisonous. Also, do not put sandpaper sleeves on the perches. Their surface is too rough for the sensitive skin of the birds' feet.

Food and water dishes: These will be part of the accessories supplied with a new cage, but usually there are not enough of them. After all, you will want to

47

PROPER CONDITIONS AND CARE

give your canaries not only birdseed and water but also fresh greens, sprouts, and perhaps egg food as well (see page 64). Plastic dishes are easy to clean and should be placed where no droppings will land in them. Cages designed to accept food dishes hung on the outside (see page 47) are especially practical.

Be careful with automatic seed dispensers. In many designs the opening can get plugged up with seed husks, so that the birds might starve even though there is plenty of food in the feeder. If you do choose an automatic feeder, make sure the opening at the bottom is wide, and check daily to make sure the seed is available to the birds.

Water bottles that can be attached to the outside so that only the drinking spout sticks into the cage are highly recommended. The water can be changed easily and hardly gets dirty at all. Don't pick too small a bottle. In hot weather, canaries need quite a lot of water. Place the bottle a few inches above a perch so that the birds can drink comfortably.

Grit or ground up seashells: Canaries need grit to help them digest their food. Grit is usually present in bird sand, but it is more hygienic for the birds to be able to eat it out of a dish rather than having to pick it up from the cage floor.

Bird sand: This is probably the material most often used as litter for the cage bottom, but you can also use quartz sand. Or, if you give your birds sand or grit in a dish, you can use other materials for the bottom, such as fine wood shavings.

Cuttlebone: This is an indispensable item because it supplies the birds with calcium and other essential minerals. Attach the cuttlebone in such a way that the birds can reach it easily from a perch.

A bathing facility: Being able to take baths is a basic necessity for canaries. Birdbaths that can be hung in the cage door work well, or you can place a flat dish with a rim about 2 inches (5 cm) high (such as a flowerpot saucer) on the bottom of a large cage or aviary. Birds often take sips of the bath water, so you should

TIP

Perches of natural wood can't be cleaned as well as smooth dowels because of the wood's rough surface. That is why natural branches should be replaced quite frequently. Arrange the perches so that no droppings will land on the lower ones from those higher up.

THE AVIARY

Spray millet is a highly prized treat.

make sure it doesn't get contaminated with droppings.

Toys: Canaries are not very interested in toys, but they happily occupy themselves with fresh twigs and leaves from fruit trees, birches, willows, poplars, and other nonpoisonous trees and shrubs. Sometimes they also seem to enjoy carrying blades of grass, raffia fibers, or pieces of cotton thread back and forth.

The Aviary

If you have enough room and want to keep a small flock of birds, your best bet is an aviary. You can buy complete, ready-to-use indoor aviaries. Some models are on rollers, so that they can easily be moved back and forth and taken to a balcony or terrace in good weather. With a width of about 40 inches (100 cm) and depth of 24 inches (60 cm) they don't take up much more room than a cage of the recommended size, but they are about 60 to 67 inches (150 to 170 cm) tall. This is enough space for four canaries, even if they are of one of the larger varieties. Such an aviary can, if it contains some plants and natural branches, become a very attractive part of your living room. If you plan to move your indoor aviary outside in the summer, make sure that it will fit through the door. The same accessories are required for an indoor aviary as for a regular cage. Pet stores generally don't have aviaries in stock but can usually order them. It may take two to three weeks for delivery.

49

PROPER CONDITIONS AND CARE

Living with Canaries

A hanging perch like the one shown here is a place birds like to fly to.

The canary cage should be located in the room where you spend most of your time—but not in the kitchen, because too many dangers lurk there. Please decide where the birds are going to live before they arrive. Their new home should be waiting for them completely equipped.

Where to Place the Cage

Probably the living room is the place where you and your birds will enjoy each other the most. Depending on your situation, however, your study or an enclosed veranda may work out better.

Characteristics of a good spot for the cage:

■ Plenty of light coming through a nearby window, but the cage should not stand in the full sun. Though sunlight is important, the birds must be able to retreat from it into the shade.

■ A height that allows the birds to sit at about eye level with people and survey the room comfortably. A lower location and activities taking place above the birds' heads make canaries nervous.

■ The cage can be put on a piece of furniture, a solid shelf on the wall, or a cage stand. For a very large cage or an indoor aviary, a stand with rollers is very practical. If you have cats, you might consider hanging the cage from the ceiling, but if you hang the cage, be sure to provide an extra safety catch so that the cage base can't suddenly become detached and drop to the ground.

■ Absence of drafts. Check for air currents with a lighted candle. Canaries get sick if exposed to drafts.

A bird with an insatiable appetite for dandelion leaves.

WHERE TO PLACE THE CAGE

PROPER CONDITIONS AND CARE

- Quiet. Birds like to be around their people, but they have extremely sensitive ears. A spot near the television, a stereo speaker, or the piano is therefore not suitable for them.
- A corner next to a window facing south or west is ideal. Here the birds are protected on two sides but get plenty of light.

Places to be avoided are: Rooms where people smoke a lot and the kitchen. Cooking vapors are bad for the birds, and there are too many other dangers in the kitchen for free-flying birds. Also keep in mind that birds can catch cold on windowsills because the change in temperature is too abrupt next to the windowpanes.

Note: The temperature in the birds' room should not fluctuate too much. Also, the room should not be too dark. If it doesn't get enough light because it faces north, for example, provide extra light with some fluorescent tubes that approximate the light spectrum of natural light. A timer is helpful for regulating when the light is switched on and off.

Can the Canary Cage Be in a Child's Room?

Basically, yes, but keep in mind:

The birds will be alone whenever the child is at school or spending time with friends. Canaries would much prefer having company, being with the child or the child's family. The answer therefore depends on how much time the child will actually spend in the room. If there are at least two canaries, they keep each other company and therefore don't get as lonely. Also keep in mind that if the child likes to listen to music full blast, the canaries can't be in the same room. The noise is too loud for them.

Any room with birds in it will get dustier than others because of the feathers, sand, and bits of spilled food. If a child is sensitive to such dust he or she should not sleep in the same room with birds.

If you have quite a few birds, you might want to devote an entire room to them. A cellar room will do for the purpose if it is dry, can be heated, and is equipped with proper lighting.

Flying Free

Birds that are not allowed

FLYING FREE

to fly develop muscle weakness, quickly grow obese, and get sick. Caged canaries have to be given the opportunity to fly frequently. Unless they live in large aviaries, all birds need several hours a day out of the cage.

The first time out is of course the most exciting. But to prevent possible mishaps you have to first eliminate some sources of danger (see table, page 56).

Wait one or two weeks before you let your birds fly free for the first time. They should have a chance to become well acquainted with their new surroundings and with you before they are encouraged to leave their cage. Don't be surprised if your canaries don't respond the minute you open the door. They are bound to be cautious and will think twice before they venture into the unknown world outside the cage. Perhaps they have hardly any previous flying experience. Don't under any circumstances try to chase the birds out! At some point they will take advantage of the open door. A perch or a bird tree in the room (see page 54) facilitates safe takeoffs and landings.

Particularly at the beginning the birds may be in no hurry to return to their cage. But don't try to catch them; that would spell the end of their trust in you. As soon as they get hungry or thirsty, they will find their way back on their own.

Seeds form the bulk of a canary's diet, but greens and juicy foods are also essential for the birds' health.

PROPER CONDITIONS AND CARE

Don't feed the birds outside of the cage. If you remove the food dishes from the cage an hour or so before you let the birds out and put them back replenished while the birds are still out, hunger will act as an incentive for the return to the cage.

The Bird Tree

When flying in the room, canaries head for high landing places, such as curtain rods, large houseplants, tall pieces of furniture, or lamps. These spots offer a good view of the surroundings. In nature, a position high off the ground also offers safety from predators.

Perches set up in the room are welcomed by the birds. Place newspapers or paper towels underneath them so you can scoop up the droppings easily. Pet stores also sell special trays to catch droppings under perches outside the cage.

A *bird tree* is the ideal destination spot for your canaries when they leave the cage. To construct one you will need:

■ A tree limb or small trunk from a nonpoisonous tree or

A bird tree like this one is not hard to construct. Add fresh branches to the tree periodically for nibbling.

THE BIRD TREE

Even children can build a bird ladder (see page 111).

You can construct individual swinging perches for all the birds yourself (see page 109).

Rocks, soil, and sand at the bottom keep the bird tree safely upright.

shrub (see page 61), about room height and with a lot of lateral branches particularly toward the top. The diameter of the branches and twigs should range from ⅓ to ⅔ of an inch (1 to 2 cm), and some should give a little and bounce so that the birds can practice keeping their balance.

■ Some extra branches may be desirable to provide additional places to perch.

■ A large flowerpot or some other decorative container with a diameter of at least 28 inches (70 cm) at the rim.

■ A heavy Christmas tree stand or a cement block with holes or a garden umbrella stand (depending on the diameter of the tree limb or trunk).

■ About 20 large stones, some soil, 11 to 22 pounds (5 to 10 kg) of bird sand or quartz sand, and raffia.

How to build it: Scrub the trunk of the bird tree well with hot water.

Mount it in the Christmas tree stand, cement block, or umbrella stand in such a way that it no longer wiggles and can't be pulled out. Put the stand with the trunk in the flowerpot and weigh it down with the stones so that it can't tip over. Fill the pot with soil and tamp the soil down firmly. Top it with a thick layer of sand and add a few decorative rocks. Then trim the side branches all around so that they don't stick out beyond the container at the bottom.

If you need additional horizontal branches they can be tied in place with raffia. Add a fresh branch with leaves or buds as often as possible. Your birds will appreciate it.

The birds' droppings will land on the sand and can be removed easily. Set up the tree far away from the cage so that the birds have farther to fly.

Houseplants

Canaries love plants. If you don't want your flowers to be nibbled on, place them out of harm's way before you let the birds out of the cage.

Of possible danger for canaries are poisonous plants like the following: primroses, boxwood, all *Dieffenbachia* species, yews, plants of the

PROPER CONDITIONS AND CARE

Recognizing and Eliminating Sources of Danger

Source	What Could Happen	How to Avoid It
Window, windowpane	Bird escapes; collides with glass: concussion, broken neck	Close windows and doors; draw curtains or lower shades; put screens on windows
Furniture close to a wall	Bird slips and slides down behind furniture	Cover space between furniture and wall
Bookshelves	Bird gets behind books and can't get out again	Shove books against wall; lay some books flat to create exits
Vases, buckets, aquariums, toilet, filled bathtub	Bird slips in and drowns	Cover or take away, if possible, while bird flies free
Candles, halogen lamps	Bird sustains burns or catches fire from the flame	Don't light candles; turn off lamp while bird flies free
Flypaper	Bird gets stuck on it, dies of fright	Remove flypaper
Poisonous plants, chemicals, cleansers, lead, cigarette butts, glues, Teflon pots	Fatal poisoning	Have no poisonous plants in bird room; don't leave cleaning materials, alcohol, medicines, cigarette butts around
Open cabinets and drawers	Bird climbs in; starves or suffocates	Close everything before letting bird out of cage
Open doors	Bird sitting on top of door gets crushed when door closes	Keep doors closed while bird flies; watch out for bird
Decorative vessels, wastebasket	Bird slips in unnoticed and can't get out again	Fill vessels with sand or newspaper; turn wastebasket upside down
Kitchen	Fatal burns from stove burners or hot pots and pans	Don't let bird in kitchen while you cook

HOUSEPLANTS

Natural tree branches provide healthy exercise for the canaries' feet.

nightshade family, narcissi, oleander, poinsettia, and many more. It should be mentioned, though, that no studies have been done to see if canaries would in fact nibble on poisonous plants and if they would suffer harm if they did. After all, many poisonous substances have a curative effect if administered in minute, homeopathic doses. In our aviaries we have for years had ivy growing, which is said to be poisonous. In the winter the birds now and then eat the leaves without showing the least negative effect. Indeed, the folk medicine of earlier times prescribed ivy as a remedy for respiratory diseases and gout.

Night Rest

Canaries like to have an undisturbed night's rest for approximately 12 hours. If you need to have lights on in the canaries' room, cover the cage with a thin cloth that lets air circulate through.

57

PROPER CONDITIONS AND CARE

A Varied Diet

Nature offers canaries an extremely wide selection of foods. Cage birds have to make do with what we give them. Even though we will never be able to duplicate nature's varied menu for our feathered friends, we have enough knowledge today to prepare a healthy and varied diet for them.

The Basic Food

Seeds containing fats and carbohydrates constitute the basic staple of canaries, their daily bread, so to speak. You can buy well-balanced birdseed mixtures ready made, or you can, of course, compose your own. Canary seed, the seed of canary grass, has to be included in any birdseed mixture for canaries. It is high in carbohydrates and relatively low in fats. At least a quarter to a third of the seed mixture should be canary seed. Usually, rape and niger seed, which are high in fats, make up about half of the seed mixture. Added to this are about 10 percent hulled oats, 5 percent hemp seed, 2 percent wheat, 2 percent Senegal millet, 2 percent lettuce seed, 2 percent poppy seed, and 2 percent linseed. In addition, you can offer thistle seed or even sunflower seed. Unhulled oats are also nutritious and can be added.

Quality of Food

When you buy birdseed, always check the date by which it should be sold. Food that is moldy, contains insect pests, or is rancid can cause severe problems with digestion, vitamin deficiencies, liver disease, or damage to the lungs.

Seed fit for the birds is smooth, shiny, clean, and free of bad smells. Taste a few of the fatty seeds, such as rape, yourself. If they are spoiled they taste rancid, whereas fresh rape has a sweet, nutty flavor.

A viability test (see sprouting recipe, page 59) will show quickly whether the food is acceptable. Over half of the seeds should sprout within 48 hours. If the sprouting rate is less you had best buy a new bag.

Sprouts

You should offer your birds sprouts throughout the year. Sprouts supply lots of vitamins, energy, and enzymes.

There should always be plenty of birdseed in the food dish. If the birds get enough exercise they will not get too fat.

SPROUTS

Sprouts are a must in the breeding season and when the birds molt.

Sprouting recipe:

■ Pour 2 teaspoons (10 ml) of birdseed (enough for two canaries) into a small plastic strainer, which you hang in a container (plastic or glass dish or canning jar) filled with lukewarm water. The water should cover the seeds.

■ After 12 hours rinse the seeds in the strainer and then hang them in fresh water for another 12 hours.

■ Rinse the swelled seeds once more well and hang the strainer in the dish but so that the sprouts are above the water. Cover the

PROPER CONDITIONS AND CARE

strainer, lightly. Air and some light should still reach the seeds.

■ The following day the sprouts begin to show. Rinse the seeds off once more, place the strainer briefly on a towel for drying, and then serve the sprouts to the birds in shallow dishes. Since sprouts spoil and turn sour easily prepare them with care and feed them to the birds promptly.

Note: You can also use a sprouting gadget (available at nature food stores) and follow the directions included with it.

Fresh Food
All canaries eagerly consume the half-ripe seeds and the leaves of many wild plants and grasses. If you collect wild plants, make sure they have not been sprayed with chemicals.

Plants canaries like: chickweed (the entire plant), dandelion (seed heads and leaves), shepherd's purse, common and English plantain, knot-

> **TIP**
>
> A practical way of serving pieces of fruit and vegetable is to use a strip of wood with nails nailed through it about 3 inches (8 cm) apart. You can impale pieces of carrot, cucumber, and so on, on the nails.

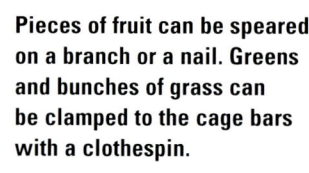

Pieces of fruit can be speared on a branch or a nail. Greens and bunches of grass can be clamped to the cage bars with a clothespin.

FRESH FOOD

Basic Menu Plan (when birds are not breeding or molting)

How Often?	How Much Per Bird?
Daily	Cuttlebone can stay in the cage all the time; wilted greens and fruit have to be removed the following morning. 2 to 3 teaspoons (10 to 15 ml) of birdseed mixture; 1 small piece of fruit, vegetable, or lettuce; 1 small bunch of greens; cuttlebone; unlimited amount of drinking water (perhaps with vitamins).
Every 2 to 3 days, alternating	(for instance, Monday: sprouts; Tuesday: soft food; Wednesday: spray millet) Remove leftover sprouts and soft food at night; leave spray millet in cage until all the kernels are eaten. 1 to 2 teaspoons (5 to 10 ml) sprouts, 1 to 2 teaspoons (5 to 10 ml) soft food, 1 millet spray, fresh branches.

Note: During the breeding season canaries need more food. They should get sprouts and soft food daily. This also applies to the molting period. The food has to be at room temperature.

weed, orache, daisy, dock, nettle, mugwort, groundsel, sow-thistle, chicory, and the panicles of many grasses.

In most climates these plants and green seeds can unfortunately not be gathered at all times of year. Think ahead to the times of dearth and freeze some of these fresh wild foods.

Unsprayed lettuce and other vegetables and fruit are also nutritious additions to the basic diet of seeds.

Vegetables: Carrots (chunks but also finely grated and mixed with soft food), cucumber, sweet peppers, zucchini, fennel, endive, corn salad, spinach, Brussel sprouts, parsley, basil, chervil, cooked potatoes, tomatoes, celery, and many others.

Fruit: Figs, grapes, raisins, apples, pears, peeled oranges, melons, tangerines, bananas, peaches, apricots, strawberries, raspberries, blackberries, cherries, rowanberries, fruit of the firethorn (*Pyracantha*).

Fresh branches: These, if they have buds or leaves, are a special treat for your canaries. Branches of the following are suitable: fruit trees, hawthorn, blackthorn, alder, oak, beech, elm, elderberry, pine, spruce, and

PROPER CONDITIONS AND CARE

blueberry bushes. In winter you can bring branches in and get them to bud by placing them in a vase in a warm room.

Don't give birds the following: Laburnum, daphne, plants of the Arum family, yew, privet, honeysuckle, monkshood, cedar, holly, oleander, deadly nightshade, foxglove, black locust, juniper, almond trees, azaleas, *Dieffenbachia* species, *Philodendron* species, raw potato, green beans, cabbage, rhubarb, grapefruit, and lemon.

These plants and their fruit can be poisonous or may not agree with birds. Of course, we know very little about how the poisons of specific plants affect various kinds of birds.

Treats and Extras

You can make your canaries very happy by giving them millet sprays now and then. Nonpoisonous leaves covered with aphids are also accepted as a great delicacy.

All fruit, lettuce leaves, and vegetables should be fresh, washed, and dried, and served at room temperature.

62

TREATS AND EXTRAS

Most canaries love fresh fruit and vegetables.

> **TIP**
>
> Buy small packages of commercial food for your canaries even though this is more expensive than buying economy sizes; otherwise the food may spoil too quickly. You should use up the food you buy within a few weeks. It is hard to store bird food properly, and important nutrients are lost over time.

Vitamin supplements (available from your veterinarian or pet stores) should be added to your canaries' food or drinking water regularly. Vitamin requirements are higher than usual during the breeding season, the molt, in hot or cold weather, and when birds are under stress or sick. Add the dosage recommended in the directions to the drinking water or to the soft food. Some white canaries, the so-called Recessive Whites, are unable to produce vitamin A themselves and therefore have to be given extra doses of this vitamin.

Minerals and trace elements are also crucial for the health of canaries. Calcium, phosphorus, potassium, and many other elements are available in sufficient amounts in cuttlebone, cooked and crushed eggshells, grit, sand, and soil.

Soft rearing or egg food is consumed eagerly by all canaries. But watch out!

PROPER CONDITIONS AND CARE

Planters for growing fresh greens, such as the one shown here, are available commercially, but the birds quickly eat them bare.

Birds put on weight quickly if they get too much of it. Offer egg food during the breeding season, while the birds are molting, and now and then in between. Like other birds, canaries feed their young a lot of animal proteins (insects). There are commercial, ready-made soft foods, to which you can add grated carrot, hard-boiled egg, cottage cheese, baby food cereal, protein drink mix, and vitamin supplements.

You may want to try the following recipe: 2 teaspoons (10 ml) commercial egg or rearing food, 1 teaspoon (5 ml) hard-boiled egg put through a strainer or crumbled fine, 1 teaspoon (5 ml) low-fat, mashed cottage cheese, a little bit of grated carrot, some fine sprouts, a pinch of cooked eggshell ground fine, a pinch of dextrose, a small pinch of a good vitamin and mineral supplement (dosage accord-

DRINKING WATER

May Canaries Have a Taste of Your Food?

Your canaries will probably be interested in just about everything you like to eat. But they should not be allowed to nibble on everything.

Be careful that they don't eat any of the following: salty and spicy food (including pretzels), cheese, sausage, butter, cream, fat, chocolate, pastries, sugar, alcohol, coffee. These substances could make your canaries very sick or even be fatal for them.

You may give them a bit of the following: fruit, bread or cake crumbs, cooked potato, vegetables, lettuce, cottage cheese, a bit of pasta, hard-boiled egg—but remember: without salt or spices.

ing to directions), and a few drops of cold-pressed oil (such as olive oil or thistle oil). You might also add some insect-based soft food or fresh insects such as aphids, water fleas, fruit flies, insect larvae, small worms, centipedes, spiders, and wheat germ, food yeast, protein granules, fine quartz sand, and algae meal.

Mix everything together into a slightly moist but still crumbly consistency and give no more than 1 to 2 teaspoons (5 to 10 ml) per bird. Parent birds rearing young should receive more. Soft food spoils very quickly, and the mixture described can be kept in the refrigerator for no more than one day.

Drinking Water

Canaries always have to have fresh water available. In hot weather they consume as much as 3 teaspoons (15 ml) per bird per day; even at normal room temperature they drink about 2 teaspoons (10 ml). Some of the water also evaporates or may get spilled. If you use tap water, let it sit for a while to reduce the chlorine. If your tap water is highly chlorinated, use noncarbonated mineral water.

Check to make sure that the drinking water does not get contaminated with droppings. The safest way is to use an automatic water dispenser.

Drinking water must never be contaminated with droppings. Make sure to change it daily.

2 PROPER CONDITIONS AND CARE

Conscientious Care

Ordinarily, canaries take care of their plumage, beak, legs, and feet themselves, spending a lot of time on it and doing an excellent job. It is up to you, however, to make sure that the cage and everything in it is in tiptop hygienic shape and that the birds are not lacking for anything. Be meticulous in the performance of the cleaning chores or germs and parasites may quickly turn up. It is best to establish a feeding and cleaning routine and stick to it. That way you are not likely to forget anything.

The Daily Bath
Canaries are true water lovers and are happiest if they can bathe every day. Baths are essential for proper conditioning of the plumage. The plumage of canaries that can't bathe regularly quickly gets dirty and disheveled. A covered birdbath that can be hung in the open cage door is most prac-

Birds go through all sorts of contortions in order to clean every last little feather on their body.

KEEPING THE CAGE CLEAN

TIP

▼

Provide perches of varying thickness so that your bird's toes and nails always come into contact with a surface as it moves around the cage. If the perches are too thin, the nails will become overgrown and will need to be trimmed.

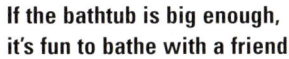

If the bathtub is big enough, it's fun to bathe with a friend.

tical and is highly recommended. Since it is enclosed on all but one side, less water gets splashed about, and the water is also better protected from droppings and dirt. In an aviary such a birdbath can simply be put on the floor. An aviary could also accommodate one of those nice, large birdbaths designed for parrots. Another alternative for a large cage or an aviary is a flat dish with a rim about 2 inches (5 cm) high, such as a clay saucer for a flowerpot.

Fill the birdbath with about 1.2 inches (3 cm) of cold to lukewarm water. Be sure the water is suitable for drinking, and don't add anything to it; birds tend to take a drink of the bath water before they immerse themselves.

If your birds spend quite a lot of time outside the cage every day, you can of course place the birdbath somewhere in the room, where the birds will be delighted to visit it.

Some birds prefer regular spraying with a plant mister to submersion baths. Give it a try with your birds and see how they react to the fine, lukewarm spray—but always use fresh water.

Note: If your birds refuse to use their "bathtub," place a lettuce leaf or other greens in it. This usually helps them overcome their reluctance to approach the unfamiliar vessel.

Keeping the Cage Clean

The best way to prevent illness is to keep the birds' living space, whether cage or aviary, in a sanitary condition. Do not use detergents or rinses when you clean, as residues of these substances can be poisonous to the birds. Hot water, a brush, and a scrubbing sponge are all that is needed. And don't use disinfectants. They only interfere with the birds' immune system and do more harm than good. You should

PROPER CONDITIONS AND CARE

Cleaning Schedule—What to Do and When

Daily	**Once or Twice a Week**	**Monthly**	**Every 3 to 6 Months**
• Remove water bottle and all food dishes; empty, wash, dry, and refill them. If you have an automatic food dispenser, check how much food is left in it. Remove empty husks. Take out wilted greens and/or branches and replace with fresh ones. Leave millet spray in cage until it is eaten bare. • Scrub away all droppings from perches, branches, and cage bars with a hard brush and wipe perches clean. • Pick up droppings and spilled food from the sand with a spoon or small trowel; add a little fresh sand if needed. • Clean birdbath and fill with fresh water. • Observe the birds—are they lively and active? • Make sure there are no bits of leftover food anywhere. • If you have breeding pairs: Do they have sufficient nesting material? Are there eggs yet? • Clean the area around the cage.	(Depending on the size of the cage and the number of birds) • Thoroughly clean everything in the cage (food dishes, food and water dispensers, perches, branches, birdbath) and the cage itself. • See if there is enough grit left and check the cuttlebone. • Attach a new millet spray if needed. • Empty sand drawer and wash it with hot water. Replenish the sand. In an aviary, replace dirt, sand, or litter that is dirty; if there is natural soil, hoe it thoroughly. Wash off stones and hose down shrubs.	• Replace natural branches. • If possible, hose down the cage in the bathtub with hot water and scrub it thoroughly. • Check cage or aviary for places that need repair. • Check all cracks and nests in the cage or aviary for signs of mites. • Trim the birds' nails if necessary (see page 70). At the same time, examine the birds for parasites. • Scrub the bird tree with a brush and wash it. Replace the top layer of sand in the container.	• Have the birds' droppings analyzed for parasites. • In outdoor aviaries, dig up the soil about spade deep; replace the surface soil with fresh earth, or change all the soil.

PERSONAL HYGIENE

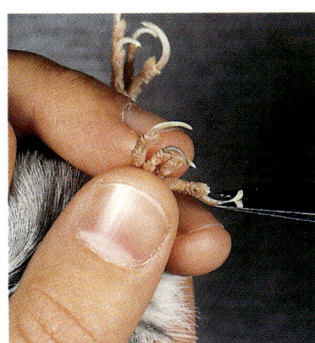

If the claws grow too long and begin to twist, it's time to trim them.

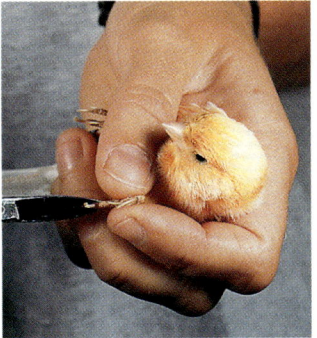

Hold the bird gently in your hand and trim the tips of the claws with nail scissors.

Wherever they perch, canaries use their flexible claws to get a good hold.

have recourse to disinfectants only if your veterinarian prescribes one to get rid of parasites or other specific disease agents, for example. Then follow the directions strictly. If you have a steam-cleaning device, you can use it to kill germs in a way that involves no poisons.

Personal Hygiene

The plumage is taken care of with great care by the birds themselves. They meticulously smooth each feather, remove any dust on it, and oil it with a secretion from the preen gland located above the base of the tail. A healthy canary's plumage is always clean, unbroken, sleek, and smooth. (The curly feathers of some type canaries are an exception.) In the course of the molt, the birds have to gradually replace their plumage because the feathers have become worn and may be damaged (see page 70).

The beak is rubbed frequently on both sides against branches and stones. That is how the canary keeps it clean. Normally the beak should be closed, solid, and smooth. Occasionally, the upper or lower mandible may grow longer than the other and thus interfere with the bird's eating. If that

PROPER CONDITIONS AND CARE

should happen, take the bird to the veterinarian promptly.

The claws usually get enough wear if there are natural branches of varying thickness in the cage. If they should grow overly long or become twisted, they have to be trimmed. Otherwise, they might get caught in something and cause the bird injury, or they may interfere with normal walking and perching.

Trim the claws with special, small claw clippers or with nail scissors. To prevent injury, it is important to hold the bird in your hand properly when doing this and to cut at an angle that follows the natural growth of the nail (see photo, page 69).

Note: Don't trim the nails too close or you might cut into the quick and hurt the bird. If bleeding occurs, stop it immediately with a styptic preparation (see page 78) because too much blood loss can lead to death.

Don't hold the bird too tightly while you operate on the claws. If too much pressure is applied to the thorax, the bird might stop breathing. If you feel insecure about trimming the claws yourself, have the veterinarian do it.

The Molt

The molt is not a disease but a perfectly normal and

Canaries like to rub their beaks on natural branches. This rids the beak of dirt and traces of food.

Canaries have no trouble balancing on one leg.

THE MOLT

Places the beak can't reach are cleaned with the help of the claws.

Canaries can turn their heads almost 180 degrees and can thus preen even the back thoroughly.

natural phase in a bird's life. However, it does put a great strain on the bird and if birds have become debilitated during the preceding breeding season, the molt can sometimes lead to problems.

Note: Canaries don't sing while they molt.

In the molt the old and often damaged feathers are replaced by new ones that grow in.

Canaries molt in late summer, after the breeding season is over. Young birds replace only the small feathers during the so-called juvenile molt. The long wing and tail feathers stay the same. Adult birds grow an entirely new plumage. Generally this takes six to eight weeks.

Canaries need a particularly nutritious diet before and during the molt. In addition to their birdseed mixture they should get lots of fresh greens, sprouts, high-quality soft food, and vitamin and mineral supplements (see A Varied Diet, page 58). Thus fortified, most canaries pass through the molt without difficulties.

Red color canaries may lose their bright red color during the molt if they have not been given enough greens and other foods high in carotenoids beforehand and don't get enough now (see Faded Plumage, page 117).

It is also important that the canaries have a lot of room and plenty of opportunity to bathe while they molt. If they get bored, juveniles in particular are sometimes tempted to pull out each other's feathers.

71

PROPER CONDITIONS AND CARE

Diseases and Preventive Measures

Greens are an important part of a healthy canary diet.

Canaries are by nature hardy cage birds. If they are housed properly, kept clean, allowed to fly a lot, and given a varied diet with plenty of fresh food, this regimen goes a long way toward keeping them healthy for a long time.

An Ounce of Prevention

In addition to offering optimal living conditions and a varied diet (see page 58) you should observe the following rules:

■ Make sure your birds get enough vitamin A. Vitamin A deficiency makes birds more susceptible to infection and is one of the most commonly encountered problems in cage birds.

■ Avoid exposing your birds to drafts, full sun, and abrupt changes in temperature. Smoky rooms and bad air in general are harmful, too. In good weather you should place the cage with the birds in it outside in a protected spot.

■ Greens you collect for your canaries have to be free of bird droppings. Don't gather plants along roadsides or where pesticides have been used.

■ If you buy a new canary to add to birds you already have, keep it quarantined for four weeks. During this time the newcomer has to be in a separate cage and not near your other birds. It may join the others only if no signs of illness appear during this period.

■ Having the droppings analyzed by the veterinarian every three to six months alerts you in good time if the birds are infected with intestinal parasites such as worms or coccidia.

■ Vaccination against canary pox provides protection against the disease and is strongly recommended for larger flocks and for birds in outdoor aviaries.

Recognizing Illnesses

Even if you try very hard to give your canaries the best of care, a bird may get sick now and then.

If that happens, it is important to realize it and act as quickly as possible because such a small bird has little reserve energy.

To add to the difficulty, birds are very good at hiding signs of illness. They may still look quite healthy when

RECOGNIZING ILLNESSES

PROPER CONDITIONS AND CARE

The Most Frequent Diseases at a Glance

What You Notice	Possible Causes and What You Can Do Yourself
Molt takes more than 1 to 2 months; plumage is dull and brittle; bald spots.	Deficiency of vitamins, minerals, and amino acids caused by incorrect, one-sided diet. Not enough exercise. Offer high-quality soft food, mixed with extra vitamins and minerals; lots of greens and carrots. Daily free flying.
Constant preening and searching in the plumage; restlessness at night.	Red bird mites, northern bird mites, feather mites, feather follicle mites, lice, or louse flies. Clean cage and surroundings thoroughly and replace litter, nesting materials, and perches. Spray birds and their environment for 3 weeks with one of the commercially available products. Increase vitamin and mineral dosage.
Runny droppings, diarrhea, dirty vent.	Agitation, stress, drop in temperature, too much fresh food, spoiled food, infection. Check food. Give birds camomile or oak bark tea to drink. Feed them hulled oats. Set up a heat lamp (see page 77).
Canary stops eating.	Unsuitable or spoiled food, infection, internal disease. Offer tempting treats, such as chickweed, dandelion, spray millet. Make sure bird is warm enough.
Shortness of breath; bird breathes with open beak.	Head cold; plugged nostrils. Keep bird warm (heat lamp), ensure high air humidity; give extra vitamins. Gently remove deposits from nostrils with a physiological table salt solution and consult your avian veterinarian immediately.
Bird sleeps during the day, plumage puffed up, apathy.	Almost always a sign of major illness. Use a heat lamp as first-aid measure (see page 77). Check the food.

DISEASES AT A GLANCE

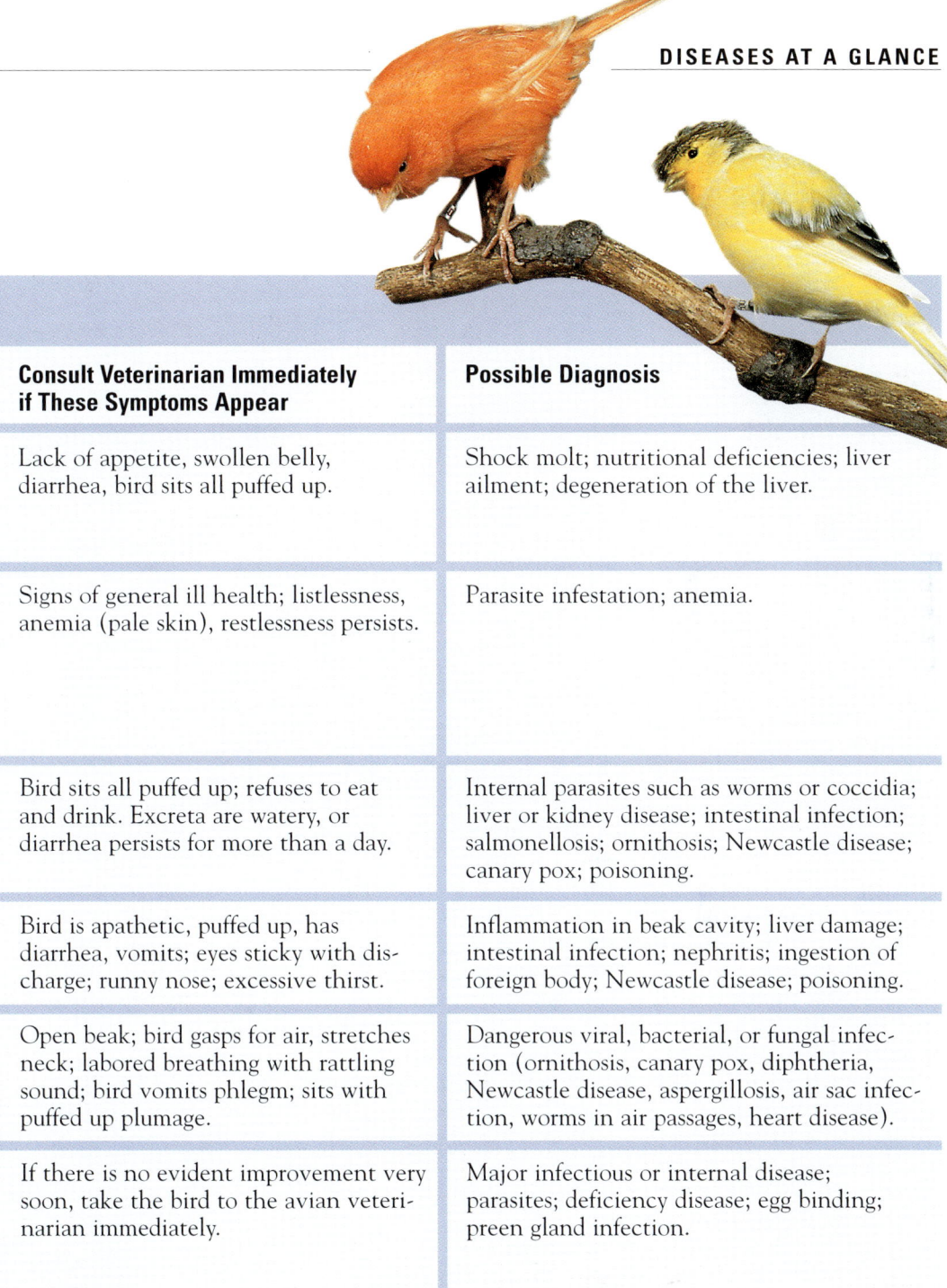

Consult Veterinarian Immediately if These Symptoms Appear	Possible Diagnosis
Lack of appetite, swollen belly, diarrhea, bird sits all puffed up.	Shock molt; nutritional deficiencies; liver ailment; degeneration of the liver.
Signs of general ill health; listlessness, anemia (pale skin), restlessness persists.	Parasite infestation; anemia.
Bird sits all puffed up; refuses to eat and drink. Excreta are watery, or diarrhea persists for more than a day.	Internal parasites such as worms or coccidia; liver or kidney disease; intestinal infection; salmonellosis; ornithosis; Newcastle disease; canary pox; poisoning.
Bird is apathetic, puffed up, has diarrhea, vomits; eyes sticky with discharge; runny nose; excessive thirst.	Inflammation in beak cavity; liver damage; intestinal infection; nephritis; ingestion of foreign body; Newcastle disease; poisoning.
Open beak; bird gasps for air, stretches neck; labored breathing with rattling sound; bird vomits phlegm; sits with puffed up plumage.	Dangerous viral, bacterial, or fungal infection (ornithosis, canary pox, diphtheria, Newcastle disease, aspergillosis, air sac infection, worms in air passages, heart disease).
If there is no evident improvement very soon, take the bird to the avian veterinarian immediately.	Major infectious or internal disease; parasites; deficiency disease; egg binding; preen gland infection.

PROPER CONDITIONS AND CARE

A fight over a nibble stick. Each bird wants to have the best spot near this delectable treat.

they are already seriously ill (see table, pages 74–75).

The state of nourishment gives a good indication of a bird's health. If you feel a bird's breast, it should be round and the muscles feel firm. The sternum should not stick out sharply.

Of course, you should not pick up a canary too often to examine it because this is very stressful for it. It is therefore all the more important to watch your birds closely.

■ Is a bird suddenly behaving differently from usual?
■ Is it not eating well?
■ Are the feathers raised or are there bald spots?
■ Does the bird sit all puffed up and on both feet during the day instead of on just one, which is the normal sleeping position?
■ Are the eyes half closed during the day? Are they dull or encased in a sticky discharge?
■ Is the head tucked in the feathers much of the day?

FIRST AID

TIP

Canaries are good at hiding most symptoms of disease. This is a natural defense strategy, for if a bird in the wild were to show weakness, it would soon fall victim to a predator. It is all the more important, therefore, to keep a watchful eye on your canaries.

Dandelion leaves contain 10 to 30 times the amount of minerals that lettuce or cucumbers do.

■ Are the droppings runny?
■ Does the beak look different from normal?
■ Is there a discharge from the nostrils? Are the nostrils plugged up?
■ Are the legs scabby or do they show welts?
■ Is the breathing labored?
■ Are the toes swollen, red, or black?
■ Is the canary unable to perch properly?
■ Is one wing hanging down, or is one leg held in an unnatural position?
■ Are there pustules or swellings anywhere on the body?
■ Is the bird restless or does it strain continually?
■ Do you see blood anywhere?

If the answer to any of these questions is "yes," your bird is sick!

First Aid

The first thing to do is to isolate the sick bird. Box cages that are open on only one side are good for this purpose, or you can construct your own with the aid of a cardboard box (see drawing, page 80). In such a box the bird will have quiet and feel safe. If the patient refuses to hop onto your hand, the best way to catch it is to darken the room, leaving only a blue or red light on. Then the bird can't see well enough to fly off and you can cautiously get a hold of it from behind. If the room can't be darkened, try to quickly throw a light cloth over the bird. It is important not to chase it long and not to put too much pressure on its chest. Make sure the bird will have peace and quiet.

If the bird looks puffed up, has a cold, or strains, warmth will be beneficial. Set up an infrared heat lamp (150 to 250 watts) about 12 to 16 inches (30 to 40 cm) from the cage (see drawing, page 80). Only part of the cage should be exposed to the light, so that the bird can retreat to a cooler spot whenever it wants to. The temperature should not rise above 95 to 104°F (35 to 40°C) in the light beam. When the patient begins to recover, the temperature

77

PROPER CONDITIONS AND CARE

should be gradually reduced by increasing the distance between the lamp and the cage. If you have no heat lamp, you can supply warmth by putting a heating pad or a hot-water bottle on the cage floor underneath the sand (see drawing, page 81). At the same time you should increase the air humidity by hanging a damp cloth on the side of or over the cage.

Bleeding should be treated immediately with ferric chloride or hydrogen peroxide. Small birds bleed to death very quickly. In most cases an avian veterinarian should be consulted as quickly as possible.

The Veterinarian

It is best to look for a veterinarian knowledgeable about birds before an emergency arises.

For the trip:

■ If possible, take the bird in its own cage (unless that is too large) or in a box cage. Don't clean the cage before you go; instead, you may want to cover the sand with clean white paper towels so that the droppings are easier to examine.

■ If there are several birds in the cage and only one seems to be sick, you should take all of them (except if they are in an aviary).

■ Throw a cloth over the cage to reduce the stress level for the bird and to keep out drafts. Avoid exposing the bird to cold.

■ Take along for examination samples of all the foods the bird eats and, if possible, some fresh droppings.

Questions to expect:

The veterinarian will ask you some questions, such as:

■ When did the symptoms first appear?

■ How old is the bird, and how long have you had it?

■ Has it had contact with other birds, including wild ones?

■ From what breeder or dealer did you get it?

■ What does it drink?

■ Is it allowed to fly free?

■ Could the bird have eaten something poisonous or inhaled noxious fumes (as from Teflon pans)?

■ Is it raising young or has it done so in the past?

■ Has this bird or any other been sick before? What was the problem then?

Stiff contour feathers form the flight feathers of the wings and tail.

THE VETERINARIAN

The yellow bird is trying to shove the white one away from the cucumber slice.

PROPER CONDITIONS AND CARE

How to Give Medication

You can't be sure that your avian patient will actually ingest medication you add to its food or water because sick birds often eat very little and refuse to drink water that doesn't taste normal. The best way to give medication therefore is to introduce it directly into the beak with an eyedropper or small plastic syringe (see drawing, page 81). This is assuming, of course, that your canary trusts you enough for you to be able to pick it up without giving it a heart attack.

Liquid vitamins can usually be added to the drinking water, and vitamin and mineral powders are best mixed into the soft food.

Diseases That Can Be Transmitted to Humans

A few infectious diseases of birds are highly contagious and dangerous to humans as well.

That is why birds showing suspicious symptoms must be isolated and taken to the veterinarian as soon as possible.

Ornithosis, also known as psittacosis (if it occurs in parrots), is caused by bacteria

The heat of an infrared lamp feels good to a canary with a cold. Set the lamp up at about 12 to 16 inches (30 to 40 cm) from the cage (see page 77).

If you don't have a box cage, you can provide the necessary peace and quiet by setting part of a cardboard box over the cage.

DISEASES THAT CAN BE TRANSMITTED TO HUMANS

A hot-water bottle buried in the sand may help a bird feel better.

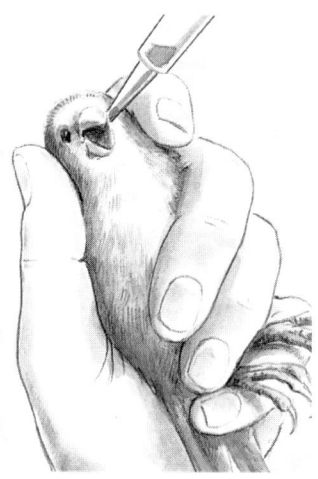

Medication is best given with a plastic syringe (without needle).

of the genus *Chlamydia*. In birds it affects primarily the eyes and respiratory system. Other signs are apathy, lack of appetite, and diarrhea.

In humans the disease can cause anything from mild flulike symptoms to severe pneumonia accompanied by high fever and violent headaches, and it may give rise to dangerous complications. Thanks to strict laws, comprehensive quarantine regulations, and effective drugs, the disease has lost much of the terror that was once associated with it.

It usually takes one to three weeks for the disease to appear after exposure, though in some cases up to three months can elapse. Canary owners should consult their physician if they have any vaguely flulike symptoms and tell him or her that they keep birds.

Humans absorb the pathogen through breathing in infected dust or through contact with the droppings of infected birds. Even canaries that are apparently healthy may secrete the pathogen.

Newcastle disease or avian pneumoencephalitis is caused by a virus. In birds the symptoms are: discharge from nostrils and eyes, breathing difficulties, and sometimes diarrhea and paralysis. Because this disease is so contagious and deadly to canaries, any incidence has to be reported. Your veterinarian will initiate the necessary procedure.

Newcastle disease rarely affects humans. However, humans can become infected through direct contact, in which case conjunctivitis, often extremely painful, develops after one to four days. Most of the time it passes quickly without adverse consequences.

Salmonellosis rarely spreads from birds to humans.

Birds in outdoor aviaries are most susceptible to this disease. The symptoms include: sitting with puffed-up plumage, diarrhea, breathing difficulties, and excessive thirst. Many infected birds die; however, some birds continually secrete the pathogen and yet appear to be healthy.

In humans the disease causes vomiting and diarrhea, and there can be complications.

2 PROPER CONDITIONS AND CARE

Canary Breeding

Surely one of the most satisfying experiences in keeping canaries is to watch a pair raise offspring. March or April, when the days are getting longer again, is the time when cock and hen are ready for their nuptials.

Choosing the Right Mate

Perhaps you already have a compatible pair of birds, but if you are still looking for a partner for your bird, select "him" or "her" in the fall or by January at the latest. What really matters is that the two birds get along well together (see Getting Canaries Used to Each Other, page 104).

Canary breeding is a science, and if you want to breed selectively for a certain color or type, or for song, you should consult an experienced breeder or join a canary club.

A few basic rules, however, are important to follow even for the hobby breeder, or else the embryos may die in the egg (lethal factor) or the offspring may be weak, sickly, or have poor plumage.

■ Never try to mate two canaries with crests, such

A canary cock is feeding his brooding mate.

WHAT THE PARENT BIRDS NEED

The young have to be a few days old before the father starts feeding them directly with food from his crop.

as Glosters. One of the breeding pair has to be uncrested (lethal factor!).

■ If you have an intensive color canary (an A bird), always combine it with a nonintensive one (a B bird).

■ You also should never let two Dominant White canaries breed because of the lethal factor.

Attempts to breed a Recessive White with a Dominant White have also proved unsuccessful.

■ Make sure that siblings or parents and offspring don't mate (inbreeding).

What the Parent Birds Need

Cage: It should be at least 32 × 24 × 16 inches (80 × 60 × 40 cm) (better yet: 40 × 24 × 22 inches [100 × 60 × 55 cm]). Box cages (enclosed on three sides) are also suitable. Ideally, all food dishes can be serviced from the outside.

Nesting aids: Breeders supply their canaries with nesting aids in February or March. These aids consist of hemispherical baskets made of bamboo, wire, or plastic mesh, in which the hen then builds her nest. Hang the basket as high as possible in a protected corner of the cage. Even better are nest baskets that can be hung from the outside—similarly to birdbaths—and have protective wire all around them.

Nesting material: The hen will line the basket artistically with suitable nesting material, such as sisal or coconut fibers, dry blades of grass, hay, dry moss, animal hair or lint; and short pieces of cotton thread (available

2 PROPER CONDITIONS AND CARE

After the nest is finished the canary hen is ready for the cock. Copulation is a tricky balancing act.

at pet stores). Don't offer just soft materials like lint; otherwise, the nest will not hold together.

Note: You can also buy preformed nest platforms made of sisal fiber or coarse felt. Animal hairs (as from dogs or sheep) should be no longer than 2 inches (5 cm) so the birds can't get entangled in them or strangle themselves.

Diet: During the three weeks before the first egg is laid, the parent birds need more food than usual. Supplement the seed mixture with plenty of greens and with egg food fortified with proteins, vitamins, and minerals during this period. After the eggs are laid and until they hatch, the food doesn't have to be quite so rich. Too much egg food would in fact be harmful at this point. As soon as the chicks have hatched, the parents' need for nutritious food high in protein rises again sharply.

COURTSHIP AND MATING

Since canaries brood in open nests, you are able to follow the development of the baby birds closely.

Courtship and Mating

With the onset of the breeding season the cock starts wooing his chosen female by singing constantly. The hen picks up a small feather or a blade of grass in her beak and flutters around excitedly. She may also encourage him with soft or quite audible calls. Sometimes he spoils her by bringing her food; she readily lets herself be fed.

Then the big moment arrives. The female is ready to mate and urges the male to mount her. She crouches down with trembling wings and raises the tail slightly. The cock flies on top of her and tries to get a hold on her back feathers. Beating his wings vigorously to keep his balance, he presses his protruding cloaca against hers, and in this way the sperm is transferred to the female's ovaries. Shortly after copulation, both birds tweet softly. Generally, the male mounts the hen

85

PROPER CONDITIONS AND CARE

several times. All this happens only after the birds have surveyed the nesting opportunities and made their choice.

Now the female starts building her nest. Sometimes the male assists by bringing nesting material, but the female is the sole builder. He supports her labor by singing as loud as he can.

The First Eggs

Two days after the soft lining of the nest is in place (and five to ten days after the lovemaking), the hen's abdomen shows a noticeable swelling. The next morning there will be a pale blue, lightly speckled egg in the nest. For the next few days a new egg will appear every morning. When there are four to six eggs, the clutch is complete.

In nature the hen waits until all the eggs are laid before brooding, but in domesticated canaries the hen usually starts sitting on the eggs as soon as the first one is laid, with the disadvantage that the first eggs hatch earlier than the later ones and the first chicks get a head start on the others.

That is why experienced breeders carefully remove each newly laid egg from the nest in midday and replace it with an artificial egg made of plaster or plastic (available at pet stores). The real eggs are returned and the fake eggs taken out again after the fourth egg is laid. This way all the chicks hatch at the same time and start life on an equal footing.

Note: A small plastic spoon works best for carefully removing the real eggs from the nest. Place the eggs in an open egg carton after padding the egg sections with cotton batting. Make sure the carton does not get

Four to six eggs at most complete a clutch for canaries.

TIP

You can check if the eggs are fertile four days after the hen starts brooding. Pick up each egg gingerly between your thumb and index finger and hold it in front of a light. A flashlight works well. The embryo shows up as a dark blob with fine, red blood vessels. Let the hen sit on her eggs even if none of them are fertile so as not to disrupt her biological rhythm.

INCUBATION

These baby canaries are seven days old. They are only lightly covered with down feathers. For the first few days the mother keeps the nest clean by promptly removing the nestlings' feces.

At two weeks the instinct to flee has developed in the chicks. If something frightens them they panic and jump out of the nest.

jolted and keep it protected from heat and cold. When the clutch is complete, return the real eggs, treating them as carefully as you did when removing them.

Incubation

The hen broods the eggs by herself; the cock does not take turns sitting on them. His task is to feed his mate from his crop. In between, he sings to her diligently.

The female leaves the nest only briefly in the morning and evening to drink and defecate. The eggs take only 13 or 14 days to hatch. When the time has come and if the eggs were fertile, each chick pokes a small hole in its shell with its *egg tooth*, a small, horny protuberance on the upper mandible. The hole is gradually enlarged until the shell breaks open. Soon, all the chicks lie in the nest, almost naked, covered with only a few down feathers. The eyes are still closed.

Development of the Chicks

The mother keeps the baby birds warm and feeds them.

2 PROPER CONDITIONS AND CARE

During the first few days she hardly leaves the nest, and it is up to the father to bring enough food for everybody. He feeds the female, and she stuffs the predigested food mush down the hatchlings' hungry beaks. The young grow very fast, and after only one week, feather quills become visible. The eyes are open by that time, too. At 12 days the baby birds are almost completely covered with feathers.

The young spend about 16 days in the nest. Then the strongest one pumps its wings and flutters to the bottom of the cage. The others soon follow.

Note: There is no legal requirement to band canaries, but all organized fanciers band their birds as proof of their lineage. Official bands or rings have to be obtained from a canary breeders' society. If you want to band your young canaries you have to do so by the time they are about a week old; it is impossible to slip the rings on later. Have a breeder show you how to do it.

The Fledglings

The young are still fed by the parents after leaving the nest, but gradually they have to learn to eat on their own. That

Twisting and stretching are part of the daily gymnastics program.

A SECOND BROOD

Why Do Canaries Have to Wash?

Have you ever watched your canaries during their daily washing routine? They go through all sorts of contortions in order to clean every feather with the beak. To make the plumage water-repellent, they rub oil over it, which they take from the preen gland at the base of the tail. The toes are used for areas beyond the beak's reach, such as the head and neck. Canaries are happiest if they can take an extensive bath every day. Make sure they always have access to a shallow bowl with fresh water. After bathing, the canaries shake themselves vigorously and then fluff up their feathers.

A canary spends many hours a day preening.

is why suitable food should be offered in a dish on the cage bottom. The beaks are still soft and delicate at this time, so the fledglings are not yet able to shell seeds. They continue to need rearing food fortified with protein, calcium, and other minerals (see page 64). Gradually, cracked seeds can be mixed in. You can crack the seeds by spreading them on a dish towel and running a rolling pin over them. The young birds should also get sprouts (see page 59) and, if possible, half-ripe seeds along with fruit and vegetables (see page 60). Don't forget fresh drinking water.

Note: If they get too much fresh food, the youngsters may get diarrhea.

When they are 30 days old, the young are completely independent. They can now be separated from their parents and should be allowed to fly as much as possible.

At six weeks, the young canaries enter the so-called juvenile *molt*, in which the small contour feathers are replaced but not the long tail and flight feathers.

A Second Brood

Shortly after the young leave the nest, the mother gets ready to build a new one and breed again. If you don't want any more baby canaries, remove all nesting materials and nest baskets from the cage.

Understanding Canaries

Canaries have been living under human care for several centuries, but they have retained many of the behavior patterns of their wild relatives. If you watch your little songsters carefully, you will learn to understand them better and increase your enjoyment of them.

UNDERSTANDING CANARIES

What Canaries Can Do

Over many generations of living with humans, canaries have become quite used to their keepers. More than any other cage bird, they let people who observe them closely share in their lives. Nevertheless, they still behave completely as birds, and it is useful to learn as much as we can about their nature.

The Senses

Vision: Canaries orient themselves primarily by the use of their relatively large eyes. Since the eyes are placed on the side of the head, canaries have a field of vision of about 300 degrees. They can see what is happening in front of them, on the sides, and diagonally in back of them. The two eyes can also rotate independently of each other and perceive images separately. Birds see in color, so it is no wonder that in many species the males are brightly colored to attract mates, but canaries hardly see at all in the dark. That is why it is important for them to have found and settled on their perch or nest by the time dusk falls.

Hearing: The auditory sense is also very highly developed in canaries. Canaries can distinguish different sequences of notes, remember them, and reproduce them. It is this ability that accounts for their learning to sing so well, to imitate other birds, and to incorporate even non-bird sounds in their song.

Sense of balance: The organ responsible for maintaining equilibrium—located in the inner ear—is also very sensitive. Canaries keep their balance effortlessly in the air and even on thin branches that whip up and down.

Smell: The olfactory sense is, however, relatively weak in birds as compared to that in dogs, for example.

Taste: Birds also have rather poorly developed taste buds. They apparently search for food primarily with their eyes. Once food is located, the taste buds along the rims of the beak determine whether it is edible. This does not mean, however, that canaries lack a sense of taste. They love sweet things, for example. And you can see over and

The secretion for oiling the feathers is taken from the preen gland.

HOW CANARIES FLY

over again that not all canaries have the same taste in food.

How Canaries Fly

Canaries are made for fast flying. Everything about them is designed for this purpose: the body structure, the organs, and the plumage.

The skeleton is extremely lightweight yet strong. Many of the bones are hollow, with air sacs extending

UNDERSTANDING CANARIES

into them. The technical term for this is pneumatization of the bones.

The flight muscles, which have an extremely active metabolism, are considered the most efficient skeletal muscle system of any vertebrates. The price paid for this efficiency is that canaries burn up about 15 times as much energy when flying as when resting.

The lungs are considerably smaller than those of mammals of comparable size yet are about ten times as efficient. Birds are able to absorb oxygen even at considerable altitudes. Several air sacs reaching deep into the abdominal cavity, between the large flight muscles, and into the skeleton are directly or indirectly connected to the bronchi. Birds breathe by raising and lowering the sternum.

The air sacs function as bellows for breathing. But they also serve as air reservoirs and help equalize pressure. In addition, they keep the hard-working muscles from overheating when the birds are flying. And finally, birds lower their spe-

Bunches of wild greens and grasses can be clamped to the cage bars with a clothespin or set in a glass like a bouquet.

94

HOW CANARIES FLY

Why Don't Canaries Fall Off Their Perches When Asleep?

Canaries usually rest on one leg when sleeping. The other leg is pulled up into the abdominal plumage, and the plumage is puffed up in a thick layer. This is how the birds keep warm. The head is turned backward and the bill tucked into the feathers. Surprisingly, canaries never fall off their perches even when fast asleep. When a bird alights on a branch, a set of muscles and tendons in the foot automatically causes the toes to clamp tightly onto the perch. The bird is thus locked in place, so to speak.

cific gravity when they expand their air sacs. When fully expanded, the air sacs can occupy up to one-fifth of the body volume.

The feathers give canaries their aerodynamically efficient outline, lend protection against cold and heat, and keep out moisture. They also form the wings and allow for steering in flight. Feathers consist of keratin. Hair, claws, and horns are made of the same substance. Birds' feathers are remarkable for their combination of stiffness and great flexibility.

The contour feathers cover the entire body of the canary, some as flight feathers, some as a covering. The largest are the wing and the tail feathers. Contour feathers are made up of a central shaft from which fine but quite stiff barbs branch out on both sides. On the sides of the barbs are even finer barbules. If you look at a feather closely you can see how these barbules interlock, thus forming a tight web, the *vane*.

Down feathers are also part of the plumage and serve to keep birds warm. The first plumage of baby birds consists entirely of down feathers. At the base of down feathers grow hairlike filoplumes, whose follicles contain fine nerve endings. Probably these hairlike feathers act somewhat like antennae, guiding the deployment of the contour feathers.

When flying, birds can adjust the flight feathers on wings and tail to the air currents so they are in whatever position is most

UNDERSTANDING CANARIES

appropriate under the prevailing conditions. Thus, birds are able to take off with ease and never miss the landing place they aim for. The shape of the wings helps them stay aloft when flying because the air has to travel farther across the convex upperside of the wing than it does across its underside. According to a law of physics, this lowers the pressure of the surrounding air on the upperside while the pressure increases underneath. The lower pressure above supplies about two-thirds of the loft, and the greater pressure below, about one-third. Because of their ability to move the tips of their feathers, birds are also better equipped than any airplane to reduce air resistance and to respond to interruptions in air currents.

How Canaries Sing

The vocal organ where the canary's beautiful song originates is called the *syrinx* and is located at the lower end of the trachea where the trachea divides to form the two bronchi. When a male canary is about to sing, one can clearly see how it stretches its neck and takes a deep breath before it bursts into song.

The canary produces sounds by stretching membranes in the syrinx and causing them to vibrate. The membranes can vibrate only while air is being expelled, yet canaries go on singing at length, apparently without pausing to take a breath. They accomplish this by expelling air rapidly at a rate of about 25 exhalations per second. Canaries are even able to vibrate the two membranes in their syrinx independently of each other and

TIP

▼

In a conflict situation, canaries assume a threatening position by spreading their wings and opening the beak wide. Usually this intimidating display is all that is needed, but occasionally two rowdies hack at each other with their beaks. If the fights continue, the two birds should be separated.

Will each bird manage to consume all of its dandelion leaf?

BODY LANGUAGE

There is nothing like a bath! This canary is having a great time splashing water onto its back. Other canaries will often tilt their heads to watch. This gesture indicates that the birds are curious, want to be scratched by their partners, or are trying to attract attention. Birds also tilt their heads to watch what is going on above or below them.

thus can sing duets all by themselves.

Body Language

Canaries communicate with their partners and others of their species not only vocally but by means of gestures and movements as well.

Whetting the bill on the perch: During and after eating and drinking, canaries clean and whet their bill by rubbing it against the perch they are sitting on (see drawing, page 98). This routine gesture also seems to play a role in communication, serving perhaps to convey appeasement or express mutual agreement.

Gaping: In young birds, opening the beak wide, or gaping, expresses a demand to be fed.

Adult canaries try to intimidate each other by opening their beaks wide and spreading their wings

97

3 UNDERSTANDING CANARIES

sideways in a conflict. Most quarrels are settled by the display of this threatening gesture (see TIP, page 96). Canaries also pant with open beak when they are hot. Moisture evaporates from the oral cavity and helps them cool down. Since feathered creatures have no sweat glands, they regulate body temperature partially through the nasal passages.

Billing and cooing: This is an expression of great affection between two canaries (see drawing, page 99). During the courtship and the brooding periods the cock feeds the hen when the two are billing. But occasionally two cocks will also bill and coo together in a gesture of mutual sympathy.

Spreading the wings: When combined with a gaping beak, spreading the wings sideways is a threatening or intimidating display (see drawing, page 99). Sometimes canaries spread one wing to stretch. Almost always the leg of the same side is extended as well. If it is very hot, the birds lift both wings to let the air get at the skin better. The underside of the wings is only sparsely covered with feathers.

Puffed-up plumage: When a canary is completely relaxed, dozing or asleep, its plumage is almost always puffed up. This keeps the bird warm—or it may just be an expression of feeling comfortable. Canaries also puff up their feathers when they are cold. However, puffed-up feathers can also be a sign of illness. You can relax if the canary is standing on one leg and is either asleep or obviously interested in what is going on

Whetting the beak not only serves to keep it clean but also can be a gesture of conciliation. When a rival is involved, and a threatening or intimidating display fails, two quarreling cocks may hack at each other with their beaks. If these fights persist, separate the birds.

BODY LANGUAGE

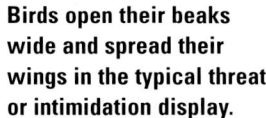

Birds open their beaks wide and spread their wings in the typical threat or intimidation display.

Billing and mutual feeding are expressions of affection.

Birds tuck their heads under their wings when sleeping so they look like feathery balls.

Stretching one leg at a time forms part of the daily gymnastic exercises.

around it. You should be seriously concerned if the bird is resting on both legs, sitting on its perch apathetically with half-closed eyes, or even squatting on the cage bottom.

Head tucked in the feathers: Canaries hide their heads in their back feathers when sleeping. They look like balls of feathers balancing on one leg. Healthy canaries rarely sleep during the day; thus, if you see a bird hide its head, this may well be a sign of illness.

Plumage sleek against the body: When canaries are too hot they sometimes press their feathers close to the body to squeeze the air out of the feathers that surround them like a pillow. But birds also sleek down their plumage when they are startled or afraid.

Shaking the feathers: After bathing and preening, canaries shake themselves to get rid of whatever dust, dirt, or water may be left and to settle the feathers in their proper places. Sometimes when canaries shake their feathers, it seems to be a gesture of embarrassment.

UNDERSTANDING CANARIES

Building Trust

In the course of domestication, canaries have gotten so used to the company of people that they have lost much of their shyness—at least compared to other finches. This does not mean, though, that they are eager to approach their keepers; rather, they are cautious and perhaps even a little timid. A canary's experiences during the first hours and days in its new home may determine whether it will become tame or remain wary. Make sure everything is ready for your birds when you bring them home.

Transition to the New Home

In most cases a canary makes the journey to the new world it is about to enter in a small cardboard box with air holes (see photo, page 46). It's dark inside the box, and the bird can hardly move, but it will sit there quietly and be less likely to get hurt than if it were transported in a cage. Of course, it will be frightened, and you should get it home as quickly as possible. Carry the box carefully, and make sure it can't tip over. Protect it against cold in winter and against heat in summer.

Tame canaries are always eager to be with their people.

HAND-TAMING CANARIES

This canary is taking food from its keeper's hand without the slightest sign of fear.

Upon arrival at home, open the box, holding it up against the opened cage door in such a way that the only exit is into the cage. Never, under any circumstances, reach into the box! If you did, the bird would be frightened of your hands forever after. If the canary refuses to come out right away, simply set the open box down in the cage. Before long, curiosity about the new surroundings will overcome fear. Usually it takes no more than a few minutes before a canary will start hopping from perch to perch, nibble on food, and preen—probably it will even chirp a bit before the day is out.

Canaries can't see at night, and it is therefore important not to disturb or startle them after dark. They don't know their way around the unfamiliar cage yet and might hurt themselves. If the room gets completely dark you should leave a small night-light on for the first night. In the morning, greet your new pets in a quiet, friendly voice. Bring fresh food and water and offer a small treat first thing. But don't reach into the cage with quick, hasty movements; keep talking to the birds reassuringly. Don't try to move your hand toward them even if they stay on their perches. After feeding the birds, move away.

Hand-taming Canaries

The way to a man's heart is through his stomach. This saying applies to canaries as well and is useful to remember when you try to win a bird's trust and teach it to become tame. Once your canary flies to your hand or shoulder whenever you call, and if it greets you in the

UNDERSTANDING CANARIES

morning with happy chirping, you will know that a friendly relationship has been established. But a warning is called for here: Tame canaries can get quite forward and fresh, perhaps pulling your hair or pecking at the food on your plate.

How your canary gets hand tame:

■ Never try to grab the bird with your hand! That could scare it half to death and would ruin the trust it has begun to develop. Only after a friendship has been built up slowly over time will you be able to pick up the bird without causing it to panic. Also, birds don't like it if their feathers are mussed.

■ Be patient! You will have to devote a lot of time to your canaries, and even then, affection can only be encouraged, never forced.

■ Watch to see which treats your canaries like best: perhaps a piece of fruit, a lettuce leaf, or a millet spray. One day, remove the food dishes after the usual morning chores but don't return them refilled with fresh food. Wait a while (no longer than 30 minutes), and then approach the cage

Can You Pet a Canary?

Birds are not cuddly animals like dogs, cats, guinea pigs, or bunny rabbits. If you reached for your canary from above to grasp it, you would scare it out of its wits. It would think that a raptor or some other predator was grabbing it. Anything approaching from above causes panicked fright. Some birds get so scared they die of a heart attack.

But if you are very patient, your canary can become very friendly and tame. It will probably fly to your hand of its own free will to get a treat such as a grape or a dandelion leaf. Never try to hold onto it when it wants to take off again; it would never trust you again. You may, however, try to scratch it gently with a small stick. Canaries like to be scratched on the side.

Maybe your canary will then soon let you pet it with your finger, and maybe it will fly to your shoulder and tickle your ear with its bill.

Remember the following: When you want your canary to perch on you, always offer it the back of your hand. Many birds are afraid of the open hand. It is *most* important to remember not to grab your bird. Doing so could destroy all of the trust that has been built up between you and your canary.

HAND-TAMING CANARIES

TIP

If you have to catch your canary for some reason—for example, to examine it for signs of illness—change your appearance enough so that your little friend won't recognize you. Put on a hat, head scarf, or glasses—something you don't usually wear. And don't talk, so that it won't recognize you by your voice. This way your bird won't associate the unpleasant experience with you.

with a favorite treat in your hand. Don't rush, and keep talking to the birds soothingly, calling them by name and whistling as usual. Slowly extend your hand a little bit through the open cage door. Don't reach in too far, so that the birds won't feel threatened. Hold the treat in such a way that the birds can approach it slowly from a perch and can peck at it without having to touch your hand. Or you can put the food down but keep your fingers near it. Now you have to be patient. Keep talking quietly, repeating the canaries' names. Torn between uncertainty and curiosity, the birds will tilt their heads sideways and then, at some point, approach the tempting morsel hop by cautious hop, to nibble at it. Now you withdraw your hand slowly and bring the birds their usual food.

■ Repeat this procedure for several days. You can soon start holding the treat with your fingers, then offer it on your hand, so that the birds have to hop onto the back of your hand to get it.

■ Even when a bird ventures onto your hand, don't attempt to pet it yet or to grab it.

■ The next step is for the birds to hop onto your arm and shoulder. This, too, is achieved most easily by means of a tempting treat. Before you know it, your feathered friends will come to you even without the incentive of food.

■ If your birds are already used to flying free regularly,

Fresh lettuce leaves are always welcome. The bird on the left has discovered them first. Will it let the other one land?

3 UNDERSTANDING CANARIES

What Canaries Like—What They Don't Like

A Canary Likes	A Canary Doesn't Like
• Another bird of the opposite sex	• Being alone, because canaries want to communicate with others of their kind
• A large, rectangular cage and much free flying	
• A spacious aviary	• Confinement to a small cage, lack of exercise, no chance to fly free
• Bathing several times a day	
• Treats, such as lots of greens, spray millet, fresh egg food	• A one-sided diet without vitamins; spoiled egg food
• Fresh branches with buds or leaves	• Poisons in the air (such as fumes from Teflon pans or cigarette smoke)
• Perches of natural branches that sway when a bird lands	• Drafts
	• Full sun without shade
• Perches high up in the room from which the canary can sing	• Dirty drinking water and inadequate hygiene
• A bird tree (see page 54)	• Cats or other pets that might try to catch it
• Sunlight and fresh air	
• Quiet surroundings	• Being grabbed or chased
• Loving humans, a familiar voice	• Major changes in surroundings
• Your not altering your appearance too much	• Shocks and vibrations
	• Noise
• Becoming hand tame	• Barking dogs
• Classical music	

you can introduce the taming exercises when they are outside their cage. Sit in the room very quietly and gradually lure the birds closer with treats. Of course it is helpful in this situation too, if the birds have had nothing to eat for a little while.

■ Canaries that are tame will always be eager for your company and will fly after you.

Getting Canaries Used to Each Other

If you have a single canary and want to give it a com-

CANARIES AND CHILDREN

Grit is essential for a canary's digestion to function properly.

panion, it is possible that the two birds won't take to each other right off. If they keep fighting and chasing each other, you will have to separate them again quickly.

The best way to proceed: Give the birds a chance to become acquainted from a distance in separate cages. Then gradually move the cages closer together until one day the birds meet face to face. The free-flying period is the best time for this direct encounter.

Canaries and Children

Canaries are a wonderful present for children. There is no better way to teach children how to treat another creature considerately and to take responsibility for its well-being. But be aware of the fact that a child's interest can often dissipate quickly.

You should make all the preparations together with your child. Clearly define the tasks—appropriate to the child's age—your child will be responsible for.

■ Children up to the age of seven should be present at and can assist with the daily chores. They should be allowed to offer special treats and can watch out for any mishaps when the birds fly free.

■ Children from eight years on can take over the daily feeding, make sure there is enough fresh water, and help with the weekly cleaning.

■ Children over ten years old can usually be entrusted with looking after the birds independently.

■ Keep in mind that the need for varied, nutritious food is especially great during the breeding season and when the birds molt. Even with older children it is probably best if you prepare sprouts and egg food yourself.

105

UNDERSTANDING CANARIES

Fun and Games with Canaries

Wild birds keep busy all day looking for food and watching out for predators. Our pet birds are largely relieved of these occupations. They get their meals served ready to eat, and even when they raise young, sufficient food is available close to the nest. So canaries are left with little to do. This runs counter to their nature. Canaries never sit still for very long; they are always in motion. That is why it is important that caged canaries be able to fly free a lot and have things to keep them occupied. Of course, if you play with your canaries, this also helps strengthen the bond of friendship and trust between you and your birds.

Keeping Your Canaries Occupied

You can give your imagination free rein when it comes to thinking up games and occupations for your canaries. Here are a few ideas to get you started:

■ Tie a thin rope (about the thickness of your little finger) inside the cage so that it forms a kind of swing. One end of the rope may be attached higher than the other. Of course, you can also hang such a rocking landing place somewhere out in the room. Your canaries will enjoy testing their balance on it.

■ Bring in branches from nonpoisonous trees and shrubs in the winter and spring and put them in a vase to bud. Be sure the vase can't tip over. The little songsters will nibble on them with great delight.

■ Place a Ping-Pong ball, a cork from a bottle, or some paper crumpled into a ball on a shelf or table the birds like to land on. Show them how these items can be set rolling or pushed over the edge to the floor. Your canaries might enjoy the game. But don't be surprised if in the future other things land on the floor, too.

■ Do you have a dog that gets along well with the canaries? Then let the birds help you brush its coat. They may think it fun to collect the dog hair and carry it to the cage.

■ You can make a thick braid of raffia and hang it in

106

KEEPING YOUR CANARIES OCCUPIED

When you are out for a walk you can easily collect a few branches to serve as perches for your canaries. Perching on natural branches keeps the birds' feet healthy.

3 UNDERSTANDING CANARIES

the cage or on the bird tree. The birds will enjoy picking out individual fibers.

■ Play classical music, good popular music, or jazz for your canaries and watch how they react. They may join in the concert.

■ Perhaps your canaries would like to take a shower instead of a bath for a change. Take a spray bottle (make sure it has not previously contained chemical substances) and fill it with lukewarm water. Then direct a fine mist at your birds. If they fly away, it is a sign that they don't like showers, but if they stay and shake their feathers, they are enjoying this new experience.

■ Give your birds a chance regularly to observe life outside and other birds from a window or from the balcony. Sometimes wild finches take an interest in caged canaries. If that happens, be sure there is a roof over the canaries so that no droppings from the wild birds can land in the cage; otherwise, your canaries might get infected with some disease.

■ Teach your birds to come to your finger or shoulder when you call and get them used to being carried around, but don't imagine that you can train them to stay there for any length of time. Canaries have to be moving constantly.

■ If you want, you can teach your canaries quite quickly to join you at the table at meal times. It is all right to let them have a bit of vegetable, potato, pasta, rice, lettuce, fruit, egg, cottage cheese, honey, or bread or cake crumbs.

A millet spray and some greens make this swinging perch even more enticing.

BUILDING A SWING

Pieces of fruit or vegetable speared on a stick of wood provide fitness training for the birds.

But don't give them anything salty, spicy, or fatty.

Building a Swing

If you have an aviary with several canaries—especially, several males—it is useful if each male has a singing perch of his own. This helps prevent fighting during the reproductive season.

Perch swings as described below (see drawing, page 55) are popular with canaries.

Take a wooden strip and drill holes in it about ¼ of an inch (1 cm) in diameter and about 8 to 12 inches (20 to 30 cm) apart. Take some smaller strips of wood (one for each hole you drilled). These should be about 8 inches (20 cm) long and ⅔ to 1 inch (2 to 3 cm) wide. Drill a ¼-inch (1-cm) hole at each end, then attach each strip to a hole in the wood with a ¼-inch

109

3 UNDERSTANDING CANARIES

(6-mm) screw and nut in such a way that the strip still moves. Stick a dowel or a twig of the right thickness (about 3½ inches [8 cm] long) into the lower hole, letting it stick out about 2¼ inches [6 cm] on one side. Make sure the dowel or twig is firmly lodged in the drilled hole so that it can't fall out. If necessary, use some wood glue. Have your horizontal wood strip long enough so that each bird can have a perch of its own. Suspend the entire contraption with thin chains from hooks screwed into the aviary roof (or the ceiling of the room).

Watching the Birds

Though there may be quite a bit of squabbling over the best feeding place, the highest singing perch, or the most desirable female, canaries are basically peaceful and congenial birds. Their sociable nature makes it possible, if you have a spacious enough aviary, to keep several male and female canaries together, even during the breeding season. It is important, though,

> **TIP**
>
> Canaries display a wide range of behavior if several are kept together. In an aviary several pairs can be combined. Granted, these birds will not become as friendly and tame as a single canary or a single pair, but the chance to observe their varied interactions will more than make up for the loss of closeness to humans.

A basket swing like this allows the canaries to refine their sense of balance.

WATCHING THE BIRDS

How to Build a Bird Ladder

It is very simple. All you need are two fairly long, straight twigs about finger thickness and a few shorter ones, some raffia, a hammer, and a few short nails. Figure out how long the ladder should be (no longer than the cage is high). Then lay the long and short twigs on a table or the floor so that together they look like a ladder. Tie them together with raffia tightly where they intersect, making sure the cross pieces can't slip out of place. You might have to nail them in place with short nails. And voilà! your ladder is finished.

The drawing on page 55 shows how the finished ladder should look. Lean the ladder against a cage wall on a slant.

and particularly at that time, that there be enough room for the birds to be able to get out of each other's way and that there be enough individual perches; otherwise, males may engage in violent air battles. Canaries that get along well sometimes even engage in mutual preening.

At the present time we have in our aviary four male canaries that have become friends. They often gather, especially in the evening, to sing as a quartet or take turns singing. Now and then, one will get himself something to eat, sometimes even sharing a morsel with a neighbor and billing with him briefly. Sometimes they visit their mates who are sitting on the nests, sing to them softly, and feed them before returning to their bachelor club.

When it gets dark they all sleep together on the same branch. Meanwhile, two of the females decided they liked the same nest, even though there were plenty of other nesting opportunities. Both deposited their eggs in the nest, and they are now sitting together on the same nest. When the males come to visit, each feeds only his own mate. I have never observed any sign of aggressive behavior between the two hens.

It is of course impossible to do selective breeding in such a community aviary. However, being able to watch the birds interact together in this type of environment is a source of great pleasure that the whole family can enjoy.

UNDERSTANDING CANARIES

Solving Problems

Most problems people run into with pet canaries are not the birds' fault. They almost always arise because the keeper doesn't know enough about the birds' basic needs and lacks the knowledge to interpret the birds' behavior correctly.

Fighting Cocks

Problems:
- There is continuous squabbling in the cage or aviary, and there are repeated air battles that send the feathers flying.
- A dominant male drives all the others away from the food dishes, the birdbath, or from the perches. If one of the other males starts singing, he is immediately attacked.
- Two cocks fight over a hen. One of them attacks his rival every time he tries to get near her.
- You have bought a pair of canaries, but the female wants nothing to do with the male.
- A subordinate bird is chased so much by the others that it is completely petrified. It no longer dares drink, eat, or sit on a perch if any of the "ruling elite" are nearby, and there is no place where it can rest in peace. Such a bird will soon die.

Causes: Canaries are peaceful by nature, and whatever conflicts arise rarely take the extreme forms described above. But during the reproductive season, from about February until summer, incidents of rivalry between males increase. If a cock starts singing, this is a challenge issued to the others. Females hardly ever get involved in these conflicts.

Normally a display of the threat posture (gaping beak and spread wings) suffices to convince an opponent to back down. This bird will fly off and try his luck elsewhere. However, in a cage or a small aviary he can't get away from the scene of conflict. Even if he gives up his claim, he is still within sight of the victor and irritates him anew by his very presence. The tension between the two antagonists has no way to dissipate.

Remedy: Either put each pair in a separate cage or get a larger aviary. In a large enough aviary you can create visual barriers between rival birds with screens, plants, or other objects. Set up a lot of high perches that will accommodate only a single bird. Minor squabbling is normal. But if serious fighting persists for weeks, the only solution is separa-

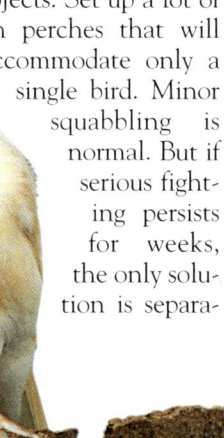

ADDING A NEW BIRD

tion, at least during the breeding period. It is also essential, of course, that there be a female for every male.

If you have a pair that doesn't get along, it sometimes helps to separate them until they are in breeding condition and then try to introduce the cock to the hen either in the evening or very early in the morning. If they still fight, you'll have to find different partners for them.

Adding a New Bird

Problem: In any established bird community there is a pecking order, and it is not easy for a new bird to fit into the group and find its way around in the new surroundings. The established birds have perches they consider their own, and each has its own territory. They will probably chase the newcomer away from the food dishes and the birdbath. Even a single bird may claim the cage as its territory and respond to a new cagemate with violent rejection.

Cause: Social birds regulate their life together through gestures of dominance and subordination, thus establishing a rank order. Canaries living in the wild have a chance to get used to each other gradually because there is plenty of room to avoid adversarial encounters and to find food somewhere else. In a cage or aviary, however, direct confrontations are inevitable. The birds have no real possibility to get out of each other's way.

Remedy: In most situations a new bird can be added to an established group of canaries without major problems, as long as this is not done during the breeding season. But the birds should first get acquainted with each other from a distance—and not just because of potential adjustment problems. It is better to keep newcomers separate for a while and observe them (see page 104) to prevent health problems from spreading to the old birds. Place the new bird or birds in a separate cage. At first the cage should be far enough away that the old and new birds can hear only each other. After a while, the cage is moved closer so that they can see each other as well and perhaps have some direct contact across

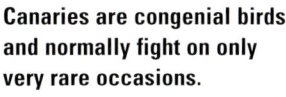

Canaries are congenial birds and normally fight on only very rare occasions.

113

UNDERSTANDING CANARIES

the cage bars. Then, after one to two weeks, you can try letting the newcomer join the other birds.

If you let your birds fly free in the room, you might let your old and new canaries meet at such a free-flying time. Another possibility is to place old and new birds together in a larger cage or an aviary, where none of them has yet established any claims.

Watch the birds carefully during the first few days to see if any problems of adjustment arise.

During the breeding season (February to July), it is better not to introduce a new male into a mixed community.

Feather Plucking

Problem: The canary mother plucks the head and neck feathers of recently fledged nestlings.

Cause: She wants to use the soft feathers to line a new nest for a second clutch of eggs. These feathers seem especially desirable to the birds even if plenty of other nesting material (coconut fiber, lint, moss, grass) is available.

Remedy: You can offer soft animal hair—dog hair or washed sheep wool, for example—and see if the hen will accept it. Probably, however, the only solution will be to separate the mother from her offspring.

Many breeders encounter this problem. When the young birds are 23 days old they can, if necessary, be

What Should You Name Your Canaries?

If you want to establish a close relationship with your canaries and have them become tame quickly, always say their names when you speak to them. Names should be short and simple so that the birds can learn them quickly. Names for canaries should contain a vowel sound such as "i" or "u" or "o" because these are sounds they themselves use in their song. Once you have chosen a name, don't change it. Here are some suggestions for names: Minny, Lilly, Kiki, Diddy, Diddle, Micky, Lulu, Tessy, Sissy, Winny, Pucky, Lissy, Jojo, Dicky, Bobo, Bibi, Girly, Frisky, Flory, Ricky. Perhaps you can come up with much prettier names of your own.

If you swoop down just right, you can drive off just about any competitor.

ABANDONING THE NEST

placed in an adjacent cage, where the parents usually still feed them across the bars. Or you can put the father and the youngsters in a neighboring cage and let him join his mate for only hours at a time.

Problem: During the juvenile molt in late summer, some of the young canaries start plucking the feathers of their siblings. The blood-filled quills of the emerging new feathers appeal to them as a treat, and eventually the youngsters pluck their fellows bare.

Cause: Initially, the young birds probably pull on the feathers out of boredom. But as soon as they develop a taste for the quills, it is impossible to break them of this bad habit. It is not clear whether some mineral or protein deficiency predisposes birds to this cannibalistic behavior.

Remedy: If there are any feather pluckers among your young birds, they have to be isolated as quickly as possible. To keep the problem from arising in the first place, you should give the birds as much space as possible. If they get lots of exercise, plenty of nutritious and varied food rich in minerals and proteins, fresh greens, branches, and bunches of wild grass to nibble on, a constantly available place for bathing, and some sisal rope and raffia tassels to play with, the adolescents will have sufficient distractions to keep the temptation from arising.

Abandoning the Nest

Problem: The female has built a beautiful nest and laid her eggs in it, but after a few days of incubating them she stops sitting on the nest. She has apparently lost interest.

Cause: The hen was probably disturbed while brooding.

Remedy: Once a hen has started brooding, make sure she has absolute peace and quiet. When you approach her, move without haste and keep talking to her reassuringly. Do only the most essential chores in the cage, and never move it, even to clean it.

Also make sure that no cats can get anywhere near the cage.

115

UNDERSTANDING CANARIES

A Canary Loses Its Mate

If a canary dies and its partner is left alone, it makes sense to get a new bird to replace the one that died. A canary should not be kept by itself. In nature, canary pairs don't necessarily stay together for life, the way cockatiels do, for example. The "widowed" bird will probably get used to a new partner quite quickly. Try to get a young bird.

If a Song Canary Stops Singing

Problem: You have a canary cock that has been singing exquisitely, but now it has suddenly fallen silent.

Cause: Canaries stop singing while they molt. At this point all their energies are absorbed in the physically demanding process of growing new feathers. Besides, they are not yet thinking about establishing a territory again or wooing a female. But when the molt is over, in the fall or winter, male canaries normally resume their song.

Remedy: If your canary still remains silent in the fall, you can try the following tricks to motivate it:
- Play some pleasant music. Canaries often try to drown out music with their own song. Sometimes the noise of the vacuum cleaner evokes the same response.
- Play records or tapes of canary songs for your bird that has become mute.
- Set up a cage with another (singing) male canary where your silent bird can hear it but not see it.
- If your song canary doesn't have a mate, get him one. Keep her in a separate cage next to his at first.
- Make sure your canary is getting a nutritious diet appropriate for canaries.

There are occasional cases, however, where a canary stops singing and remains silent for the rest of its life.

Escaping

Problem: Your canary has escaped through an open window while flying free in the room.

Remedy: There are all kinds of dangers for birds flying free in the rooms of our homes (see table, page 56)—dangers we are usually quite unaware of. Thousands of pet birds escape every year because a window was inadvertently left open. If these birds don't find a new home quickly, they are not likely to survive for long. Canaries are an easy prey for raptors, cats, and dogs, or they may starve or freeze to death. But don't try to chase after an escaped bird; it would only try to get away all the faster. Even though an escaped bird is unlikely to return, you should put the cage in the open window or on the balcony or terrace and try to lure your canary back by calling it and displaying treats.

Many a bird has also met its death by flying into a window. Canaries are instinctively drawn to the light, and they don't know that there is an invisible barrier between inside and outside. They learn about windows only slowly, and when they get scared, they will forget and fly against the glass again. That is why you should take the precaution of covering windows with curtains, cloths, window shades, or screens.

Faded Plumage

Problem: The original gorgeously bright plumage of yellow and red color canaries has gradually paled.
Cause: The birds have not been getting enough carotenoids in their food. Yellow and red color canaries have to get these substances in their food for their bodies to manufacture the lipochromes (see page 38) that will be deposited in the papillae of the feather follicles at molting time.
Remedy: Canaries can develop uniform coloration only if they get an optimal diet that includes fresh greens and carrots. Breeders of red canaries often add paprika (mild), red fruits, synthetic canthaxanthin (available at pet stores), or beta carotene to the soft food of their birds in order to make sure the plumage will be a uniform bright red.

Egg Binding

Problem: The canary hen sits on the nest motionless and with puffed-up plumage, clearly unable to pass the egg.
Cause: The hen is suffering from egg binding. This is most likely to happen if the bird did not get enough calcium before the onset of the breeding season and the eggs, therefore, lack a hard outer shell. The contractions of the muscles are unable to press out the soft egg, which remains stuck in the cloaca. Young or weakened females sometimes have difficulties passing a normal egg.
Remedy: Take the female to the veterinarian as quickly as possible. If something is not done promptly, the bird will die. Trying to take care of the problem yourself is not recommended.

The red canary has eaten his fill and is willing to cede his place to the other bird.

MY CANARY

My Canary

This is the place for your favorite photo.

_____

Name

MY CANARY

Birthdate

Breeder/Pet Shop

Sex

Breed/Color

Band Number

Special Characteristics

Favorite Food

What My Canary Likes to Do

Veterinarian's Name and Address

INDEX

Abandoning the nest, 115
Activities, 106–111
Adding new birds, 113–114
AFA *Watchbird*, 125
Age considerations, 28–30
Air sacs, 94–95
American:
  Federation of Aviculture, 125
  Norwich Society, 125
  Singer, 36–37
  Singers Club, 125
Ancestors, 12
Anemia, 75
Aphids, 62
Association of Avian Veterinarians, 125
Associations, 125
Austria, 16
Aviary, 49
Azores, 9

Balance, 92
Bands, 29
Bathing, 48–49, 66–67, 97
Beak, 69–70
Behavior, 12, 92–99
  healthy, 31
Belgian:
  Bult, 40
  Waterslager, 35
Bernese, 41

Bill, whetting, 97
Billing, 98
Binding, egg, 117
Bird:
  Clubs of America, 125
  sand, 48
  sitters, 23
  Talk, 125
  Times, 125
  tree, 54–55
Black siskins, 38
Bleeding, 78
Body language, 97–99
Books, 125
Border:
  Canary, 41
  Fancy, 38
Branches, fresh, 61–62
Breast, healthy, 31
Breeders, 26–27
Breeding, 82–89
  cage, 83
  clutches, number, 13
  diet, 84
  responsible, 32
Brooding, 87
Bullfinches, 38
Buying *See*: Purchasing

Cage, 44–45
  accessories, 46–49
  bars, 44–45
  breeding, 83
  cleaning, 67–69
  location, 50, 52
  shape, 44

  size, 44
Canary Islands, 8–9
Cape Verde, 9
Carduelis carduelis, 22–23, 39
Care, 44–89
Cats, interactions with, 22
Chick development, 13–14, 87–89
Children, interactions with, 25, 52, 105
Chlamydia, 81
Claws, trimming, 69–70
Cloaca, healthy, 31
Cleaning schedule, 68
Cocks, fighting, 112–113
Colors, 32–41
Condominiums, legal issues, 24
Contour feathers, 95
Contracts, purchase, 24–25
Cooing, 98
Courtship, 85–86
  display flights, 12
Crestbred, 41
Crested Canary, 41
Cuttlebone, 46, 48

Dangers, 56
Deficiencies, 74–75
Diet, 58–65
  foods to avoid, 65
  supplements, 63
  wild canaries, 10

INDEX

Diseases, 72–77
  transmissable to humans, 80–81
Dogs, interactions with, 22
Down feathers, 95
Drafts, 50
Droppings, healthy, 31

Egg(s), 86–87
  binding, 117
  fertility, checking, 86
  food, 63–65, 84
  tooth, 13, 87
England, 15
Equipment, 44–49
Escaping, 116–117
European goldfinch, 22–23
Eyes, healthy, 31 See also: Vision

Feathers, 95
  contour, 95
  down, 95
  flight, 95–96
  plucking, 114–115

shaking, 99
  See also: Plumage
Feeding, 58–65
Fife, 41
  Fancy, 38
Fighting, 112–113
Fiorino, 40
First Aid, 77–78
Fledglings, 88–89
Flight, 52–54, 93–96
  feathers, 95–96
Food, 58–62
  to avoid, 65
  dishes, 47–48
  dispensers, 46, 48
  egg, 63–65, 84
  fresh, 60–62, 64
France, 15
Free flight, 52–54
Frills, 39–40
Fruit, 61

Games, 106–111
Gaping, 97–98

Gender considerations, 19–21
German Crest, 39, 41
Gibber Italicus, 32, 40
Giboso Espanol, 40
Gloster:
  Consort, 40–41
  Corona, 40–41
Gomera, 9
Grand Canary, 9
Grit, 48, 105

Habitat, wild canaries, 10
Hand taming, 101–104
Harz Roller, 17, 34
Hazards, 56
Health:
  assessment, 30–31
  care, prevention, 72
Hearing, 92
Hens, 19–20

Canaries are especially fond of juicy fruits.

121

INDEX

Hierro, 9
History, 8–12
Homecoming, 31
Houseplants, 55–57
Hybrids, 39
Hygiene, 69–70

Illnesses, recognizing, 72–73
Inbreeding, 83
Incubation, 87
Infections, 74–75
International Aviculturists Society, 125
Isolation, 21–22
Italy, 15–16

Japanese Hoso, 40
Juvenile molt, 89, 115

La Palma, 9
Ladder, 55, 111
Lancashire, 41
  Plainhead, 41
Legal considerations, 24–25
Legs, healthy, 31
Lethal factor, 82–83
Light, 38
Lipochrome, 38
Liver ailment, 75
Longevity, 18
Lost-and-found, 25
Lungs, 94

Madeira Islands, 9
Magazines, 125
Mail order, 27
Makige, 40
Mate selection, 82–83
Mating, 85–86
  preparation, 10–13
Medication, administering, 80
Mehringer Frills, 40
Melanin, 38–39
Menu, 61
Minerals, 63
Mites, 74–75
Molt, 70–71
  juvenile, 89, 115
  shock, 74–75
Monks, Spanish, 15
Munchener, 40
Muscles, 94

A chat over some lettuce leaves.

INDEX

Nails, trimming, 69–70
Names, 114
Natural environment, 8–9
Nest:
　abandoning, 115
　location, 11
Nesting, 12–13
　material, 83–84
Newcastle disease, 75, 81
Newsletters, 125
Night rest, 57
Northern Dutch, 40
Norwich, 41
Nostrils, healthy, 31
Nutrition, 58–65
　minerals, 63
　trace elements, 63
　vitamins, 63

Ornithosis, 80–81
Ownership considerations, 8–41

Padovan, 40
Parasites, 74–75
Parisian, 40–41
　Frill, 41
Perches, 46–48, 50–51
Pet stores, 26
Pets, interactions with, 22–23

Plants:
　dietary, 60–61
　poisonous, 55–57, 62
Plumage, 12, 31, 69
　faded, 117
　puffed-up, 98–99
Poisoning, 55–57
Preferences, 104
Problem solving, 112–117
Purchase contracts, 24–25
Purchasing:
　considerations, 26–31
　timing, 28
　tip, 16

Raza Espanola, 41
Record keeping, 118–119
Rhinelander, 40
Rodents, interactions with, 22
Russia, 16

Safety considerations, 55–56
Salmonellosis, 81
Sankt Andreasberg, 17
Scarlet grosbeaks, 38
Scotch Fancy, 40
Seed, 58
　dispensers, 46, 48
Selection, tip, 16
Senses, 92–93

Serinus:
　canaria, 12
　serinus, 12, 22
Sex, determining, 20–21
Shock molt, 74–75
Singing, 15, 96–97
　loss of, 116
　training, 15
Size, 12
Skeleton, 93–94
Smell, 92
Social considerations, 21–22
　adding new birds, 113–114
Solitary confinement, 21–22
Song canaries, 34–37
Sources, 26–27
Southern Dutch Frill, 40
Spain, 15–16
Spanish Timbrado, 36
Species, protection, 24
Sprouts, 58–60
Stafford Canary Club of America, 125
Supplements, 63
Supplies, 44–49
Swing, building, 109–110
Swiss Frill, 40
Syrinx, 96

Taming, hand, 101–104
Taste, 92–93
Tenants, legal considerations, 24

123

INDEX

Tenerif, 9
Time requirements, 18
Tooth, egg, 13, 87
Toys, 49
Trace elements, 63
Travel box, 46–47
Treats, 62
Tree, bird, 54–55
Turkey, 16
Type canaries, 39–41
Tyrol, 16

Vane, 95
Varieties, 21, 32–41
Vegetables, 61
Veterinarian, 78, 125
Vision, 92
 night, 101
Vitamins, 63

Water, 25, 65
 dishes, 47–48
 dispensers, 46, 48
Waterslager, 35
Widowhood, 116
Wild canaries, 9–10
Wing spreading, 98
World of Birds, 125

Yorkshire, 41

Canaries never grow tired of spray millet.

USEFUL ADDRESSES AND LITERATURE

Associations, Organizations, and Clubs

A bird lover still needs years of experience to be a bird expert. And even a bird expert doesn't hesitate to ask advice and seek the help of an avian veterinarian. If an avian veterinarian is not available in your immediate area, write to the following organization for names of veterinarians who work with birds:

Association of Avian
  Veterinarians
P.O. Box 811720
Boca Raton, FL 33481-1720
Tel.: (561) 393-8901
Fax: (561) 393-8902
Web site: http://
  www.upatsix.com/aav/

Here are some other addresses that you might find useful:

American Federation of
  Aviculture
P.O. Box 56218
Phoenix, AZ 85079-6218
(602) 484-0931

American Norwich
  Society
Will and Lee Burdett
113 Murphy Road
Winter Springs, FL 32708

American Singers Club, Inc.
Clayton C. Beegle
Route 1, Box 186B
Ridgeley, WV 26753-9718
(304) 738-1689

Bird Clubs of America
Dick Ivy
P.O. Box 2005
Yorktown, VA 23692
(804) 898-5090

International Aviculturists
  Society
P.O. Box 280383
Memphis, TN 38168
(901) 872-7612

Stafford Canary Club of
  America
George E. Gray
687 Westvaco Road
Highway 51 South
Wickliffe, KY 42087
(502) 335-3513

Books

Axelson, D. *Caring for Your Pet Bird*. New York: Sterling Publishing, 1989.
Burgmann, Petra. *Feeding Your Pet Bird*. Hauppauge, NY: Barron's Educational Series, Inc., 1993.
Gallerstein, Gary A. *The Complete Bird Owner's Handbook*. New York: Howell Book House, 1994.

von Frisch, Otto. *Canaries*. Hauppauge, NY: Barron's Educational Series, Inc., 1999.
Vriends, Matthew M. *Hand-feeding and Raising Baby Birds*. Hauppauge, NY: Barron's Educational Series, Inc., 1996.

Magazines and Newsletters

AFA Watchbird
P.O. Box 56218
Phoenix, AZ 85079-6218
(602) 484-0931

Bird Talk
P.O. Box 6050
Mission Viejo, CA 92690
Tel.: (714) 855-8822
Fax: (714) 855-0654

Bird Times
7-L Dundas Circle
Greensboro, NC 27407
Tel.: (336) 292-4047
Fax: (336) 292-4272
Web site: http://www.
  birdtimes.com

World of Birds
850 Park Avenue
Monterey, CA 93940
(800) 864-2500

INFORMATION

The Author
Sigrun Rittrich-Dorenkamp is a journalist and editor who has been working for a number of magazines and newspapers. Canaries are one of her areas of specialty.

The Photographer
Most of the photos in this book were taken by Uwe Anders. He has a degree in biology and works as a freelance nature photographer and as a cameraman for nature films. Other photographers: Angermayer/Reinhard: page 37, above, right; Bielfeld: pages 35, above, left; 37, below: 40, below; Reinhard: pages 32–33; 34; 35, above, right; 37, above, left; 40, above left and right; 41, right.

The Artist
Renate Holzner is a versatile freelance artist who lives in Regensburg, Germany.

Acknowledgments
Translated from the German by Rita and Robert Kimber. Consulting editor: Matthew M. Vriends, Ph.D.

© Copyright 1999 by Barron's Educational Series, Inc.
© Copyright 1998 Grafe und Unzer Verlag GmbH, Munich
Original title of the book in German is *Der Kanarienvogel*

All rights reserved.
No part of this book may be reproduced in any form, by photostat, microfilm, xerography, or any other means, or incorporated into any information retrieval system, electronic or mechanical, without the written permission of the copyright owner.

All inquiries should be addressed to:
Barron's Educational Series, Inc.
250 Wireless Boulevard
Hauppauge, NY 11788
http://www.barronseduc.com

Library of Congress Catalog Card No. 99-27198

International Standard Book No. 0-7641-5208-4

Library of Congress Cataloging-in Publication Data
Rittrich-Dorenkamp, Sigrun.
 [Kanarienvogel. English]
 Canaries : how to keep them, feeding them correctly, understanding their behavior / Sigrun Rittrich-Dorenkamp ; photographs, Uwe Anders ; illustrations , Renate Holzner.
   p.   cm. — (Family pet series)
 Includes bibliographical references (p.   ) and index.
 ISBN 0-7641-5208-4
 1. Canaries. I. Title. II. Series: Family pet.
SF463.R57 1999   99-27198
636.6'8625—dc21   CIP

Printed in Hong Kong

9 8 7 6 5 4 3 2 1

Photos on Covers and Within Text:
Front cover: Yellow color canary (big photo); a hybrid (small photo). Pages 2–3: Canaries in a palette of colors. Pages 6–7: Canaries are elegant flyers. Pages 42–43: Busily collecting materials for a nest. Pages 90–91: Fighting over food. Back cover: Red color canary.

IMPORTANT NOTE

Important Note

This book deals with keeping and caring for canaries.

People who are allergic to feathers or feather dust should not keep birds. If you are not sure, consult your doctor before getting birds.

At this time, ornithosis is very rare among canaries (see page 80), but if it occurs it can be life-threatening to both canaries and humans. If you have the slightest suspicion, take the canary to the veterinarian and, if you yourself have cold or flulike symptoms, see your doctor and mention that you have birds.

Answers to the Canary Quiz (inside back cover)

1a (Photo on page 66 and Personal Hygiene, page 69)
2b (Photo on page 82 and Courtship and Mating, page 85)
3b (Body Language, page 97)
4a (The Daily Bath, page 66, and photo on page 67)
5b (Incubation, page 87, and Development of the Chicks, page 87)
6b (What the Parent Birds Need, page 83)
7a (Fresh Food, page 60)
8a (Incubation, page 87)
9a (Cage Accessories, page 46)

Assembly for a communal concert during the early evening hours.

636.68625
R
Rittrich-Dorenkamp, Sigrun.
Canaries.
1295

Henry Waldinger Memorial Library
Valley Stream, New York
Phone: 825-6422

DO NOT TOUCH THE DATE CARD

VS